NINJA
MIND
CONTROL

NINJA
MIND
CONTROL

ASHIDA KIM

Citadel Press
Kensington Publishing Corp.
www.kensingtonbooks.com

CITADEL PRESS books are published by

Kensington Publishing Corp.
850 Third Avenue
New York, NY 10022

All Kensington titles, imprints, and distributed lines are available at special quantity discounts for bulk purchases for sales promotions, premiums, fund raising, educational, or institutional use. Special book excerpts or customized printings can also be created to fit specific needs. For details, write or phone the office of the Kensington special sales manager: Kensington Publishing Corp., 850 Third Avenue, New York, NY 10022, attn: Special Sales Department, phone 1-800-221-2647.

Kensington and the K logo Reg. U.S. Pat. & TM Office
Citadel Press is a trademark of Kensington Publishing Corp.

First printing 1986

20 19 18 17 16 15 14 13 12 11

Printed in the United States of America

ISBN 0-8065-0997-X

Contents

Introduction

"There are no extraordinary men, only ordinary men in extraordinary situations."

Those who have purchased this volume with the idea of employing mind control to further their own selfish motives will be sadly disappointed. Indeed, such manipulations would be considered by some to be "black magic," and thus "evil." Such attempts will almost certainly bring about the self-inflicted downfall of the perpetrator.

What we shall teach is far more valuable: You shall learn how to control your own mind. You are about to participate in a great adventure. You are about to experience the awe and mystery that reach from the inner sanctum of the mind to the outer limits of reality.

These pages contain the most profound and ancient exercises ever recorded. Do not begin them lightly, or without proper respect, for they are powerful in the extreme and will almost certainly change your life for the better. Once begun, there can be no going back to the past, or leaping forward into the future. There is only the reality of now.

These movements will balance the flow of energy in the body, thereby healing old wounds and filling the self with vitality. That is their first benefit. It is often said, "What good are all the treasures of the earth, if one does not have health?" These exercises will give you health.

This will not happen immediately, of course. The effects of all yogic postures, like those of meditation, are cumulative. One simply starts, and before long, one notices that some ache or pain, which was obvious at the outset, now seems much improved or has vanished altogether. Surely these rewards of daily exercise, the maintenance and well-being of the body, are worth a few minutes of time. Surely you did not expect to read one chapter and have instant mind control over the masses. Whatever effort would have been expended toward that goal can much better be spent on the improvement of oneself; that is a far nobler mission, to be certain.

The second benefit of these techniques is the gradual development of the ability to direct, or conversely, to act in accordance with, the flow of energy within the physical body. With this power, one transcends the lower levels of consciousness that impede progress toward the realization of one's true nature and place in the universe.

Once we have acquired self-knowledge and understand the way of Nature, it is clearly evident that no one can control the actions of another. In fact, if we can learn to control our own wants and needs, let alone our fears and desires, we shall have accomplished a great deal. When that is achieved, we shall no longer seek to control others, or even to interfere in their lives by giving advice. We shall glow with the vitality and energy of inner peace.

Seeking only to improve ourselves, we shall be seen as good examples to follow; and divesting ourselves of petty ambition in order to pursue this great goal, we·shall be known as followers of peace. Because we know our inner strength cannot be threatened, we are unlikely to feel the need for power over others. In this way, the true power can be achieved, because others, motivated by self-interest, will want to know how we can do the things we shall learn herein. And when they ask, we must tell them freely, and share all that we have, so that they, too, can find the Way.

Kinjiru, pronounced "ken-jeh-roo," is Japanese for "forbidden" or "secret." Beware, those who would journey here. Beware, those who would begin the inner quest in search of the Light, for there are dangers here. You will meet creatures of the id, the masks of ego. Dare you pass between the pillars of self-doubt and gaze into the mirror of self-knowledge? These techniques can light the path for you, where many have gone before. They can lead the way to the source, where all questions are answered and all things made clear. There is power here, enough to destroy you; there is love here, enough to make you immortal; and there is wisdom here, which is knowing the difference.

The key is practice. Wisdom may come in a day, in a single flash of insight; or it may grow slowly over the years—but come it will. A journey of a thousand miles begins with a single step. The journey does not end until *you* concede that you have reached your goal.

1.
The Warrior-Mystic: Levels of Training

To be a Ninja is to be a warrior-mystic. The meaning of this term is contained in the saying, "To be a Ninja, one must be strong; one must know; one must dare; and one must keep silent."

ONE MUST BE STRONG

The principal attribute of a warrior is strength. There are two kinds of strength, the outer and the inner. The outer strength is apparent and fades with age; while the inner is subtle, unseen, and eternal. The Ninja may be possessed of either.

Normally, the strongest individual will be the leader in any group of Ninja with a similarity of purpose. This occurs naturally and without need for contest. Having trained and studied in the martial arts for long periods, the Ninja are considered masters of weaponry. Furthermore, their skill and versatility are so great that virtually anything can be employed as an implement of destruction. This does not even take into account the Ninja's lethal use of the hands and feet.

The Ninja have both fighting ability and a high level of extrasensory acuity, which grants them a psychological as well as physical "edge" in any combat. They not only possess the "strength of ten because their hearts are pure," but their calm in the face of the storm often determines the outcome. All Ninja are men of peace, and must always remain so or lose many of the special powers they have developed.

Beyond this, the Ninja are also adept at fieldcraft, infiltrating, and espionage. Because of their scouting skills and peripheral kinesthetic sensitivity, Ninja customarily surprise their opponents slightly more than half the time. This may be a result of creeping up on the enemy and striking from behind, or of using a feint or sucker punch when fighting head-on. Much of this ability is due to constant and rigorous training, as well as a vast amount of study. After that, the Ninja creates his own form.

Other benefits of being a Ninja warrior include the power to size up an opponent by his stance, and the concurrent knack of reading the body language of others, which enables the Ninja to determine the covert goal of an individual. By these means, the Ninja develops a sphere of influence within which relative safety can be maintained.

Ninja also have the ability to treat their own wounds, the minor injuries that are incurred by even the most scrupulous and careful practitioner in the course of training. With that, they also have the power to help others. Most common ailments are avoided by virtue of regular exercise and attention to diet, so good health follows naturally.

After a certain level of experience has been attained, the Ninja gains the ability to employ powers that in many circles would be considered almost psychic. The charisma of such a fighter is such that he attracts to himself, without effort, a body of followers. These followers may appear as students or associates, and they are completely loyal upon initiation. They may band together for a common goal or seek counsel; but in either event, they will remain loyal only as long as the behavior of the leader is constant.

ONE MUST KNOW

To develop the talents associated with the mystic side of Ninja training, in addition to possessing strength, one must "know." To know means to have intelligence. This does not refer to the I.Q. so often quoted as a measure of intellect, but rather to an understanding or ability to learn.

Many people limit themselves to leading boring, dull lives by accepting the judgment of others that they are of low intelligence. This is not so. Just because one does not process sensory information and replay it the same way as everyone else—which in any case would be boring in the extreme and mark the extinction of creativity—does not mean that there is a lack of comprehension or interest. Just because a person does not understand another's purpose does not mean that he is confused.

The Ninja possess mental powers of an informational, offensive, or defensive nature; but it is only during the latter stages of training that these techniques actually become effective in hand-to-hand combat. That is to say, after much practice one is able to defeat the enemy without physical contact. By that time, the student has mostly transcended motives that would land him in a situation where these paranormal powers would be warranted.

Ninja mysticism may take many forms. The simple form makes it possible to deflect negative vibrations and defend oneself against psychological assault merely by maintaining one's emotional balance. The more complex forms require mantras, somatic components, and elaborate rituals for maximum efficiency. The individual must first determine the methodology of his or her own psychological thought forms or constructs. Since one of the primary attributes of the spy has always been a good memory, most agents have never written down their techniques, although some *tora-maki,* or sacred scrolls, do exist.

Through the study of the mind, the Ninja hopes to gain wisdom and become a man of knowledge. As such, he attains an almost spiritual level of dedication to his art, which confers upon him a high degree of skill at arms. Many such accomplished Ninja are known by the eternal symbols they have adopted to signify their quests, but in time even these are put aside. At this level, the reverence for life becomes so great that the Ninja will no longer kill, and their powers are directed only toward revitalizing, protecting, and encouraging the efforts of others.

The goal of the true seeker is to become a sage, or superior man. There are certain immutable laws of the universe, which the sage must be in harmony with. Different Ninja sects espouse some laws in particular, according them greater significance than the others. But each law is essential in its own right, and must be considered equal to the rest.

The Law of Balance. Even the most ancient sages have pointed out that all things are possessed of an equal and opposite counterbalancing force in reality. The high rests upon the low; the front follows the back. One can know beauty as beauty only because there is ugliness.

The Law of Extremes. When two counterbalancing forces are carried to their limits, they are seen to be identical. One is blinded by a brilliant light as effectively as by darkness.

The Law of Karma. All things are interrelated, and everything affects everything else. Thus whatever we send into the lives of others comes back into our own life, with threefold strength.

The Law of Change. All things proceed sequentially through an orderly series of progressive steps. The one thing that can be depended upon to remain constant is that things will continue to change in a logical and cyclical manner.

A Ninja who has attained the level of sage is so at peace and in harmony with the way of Nature that he remains virtually untouched by the passage of time or the change of regimes. Such a warrior views *Yin* and *Yang* as balancing forces of the universe and recognizes the endless cycle of change, inevitable and inexorable.

The sage communicates with the Hidden Masters (see Chapter 9) and is in touch with the "cosmic consciousness" by means of his ability to direct, or flow in harmony with, the psychokinetic energy of the mind and body as one. This is spoken of in many arts, but is achieved by few. It is often known as channeling the *chi,* or vital life force. Thus it may be said that the superior man has a secret language of his own, and can communicate by telepathic means.

This level of skill is so high that there are seldom more than a few such masters known in any one generation. They rarely live in or near cities, preferring the solitude of rural or ascetic settings. They have been known to "interfere" in the affairs of men from time to time, however. This is the basis for the legends of the Old Man of the Mountain, a figure that recurs in both Chinese and medieval stories and mythology.

By virtue of their simple, monastic existence, the sages are readily able to find or manufacture for themselves almost any item or device necessary for their survival. They are patient and diligent, and they are generally considered excellent craftsmen and gracious hosts. Because of their highly developed senses and their perception of the foibles of mankind, they often appear to embody, or to have, what might be considered supernatural powers.

Unlike the Ninja who have accomplished the lower stages, the superior man attracts no band of followers, imparting to each pilgrim enough knowledge at one time that prolonged study with the sage is unnecessary.

ONE MUST DARE

The third requirement for the avid Ninja is to "dare." This refers to the Ninjas' talents and abilities that allow them to overcome the enemy with nonviolence. The Ninja at this level are the agents in the field who are masters of the bloodless coup, those who win without fighting, the magicians of ninjitsu. Dexterity is their trademark; prestidigitation, or sleight of hand, is the principle of their magical working. While the warrior contends with force and strength, the mystic battles with cunning and stealth. These attributes comprise the Ninja art of invisibility.

In ninjitsu, dexterity is as much mental as physical. To this end, agents practice codes and ciphers in addition to other mental gymnastics, such as puzzles or mazes. This enables practitioners to open all manner of locks and pass unhindered through areas loaded with traps and death-dealing devices. The Ninjas' level of skill is determined by individual cleverness and a thorough knowledge of such devices. Much of this skill also depends on astute powers of observation and an understanding of basic motivations and social patterns.

By these means, and the ability to remain unseen, the Ninja have gained a reputation for invisibility.

In practical application, such techniques depend largely upon methods of concealing oneself in shadows or other inconspicuous cover. The Ninja must also maintain adequate balance to enable him to move silently from one point of hiding to another without detection. A useful adjunct to this type of activity is wall-climbing kung, a technique which enables the Ninja to ascend vertical surfaces quickly and quietly—a practical method of vanishing from view and danger.

The primary function of the Ninja is spying, gathering intelligence either for his own use or for the purpose of espionage. Anyone may be recruited as a spy, given sufficient incentives, either of financial reward or threat of harm. Depending on the difficulty of the assignment, fees may be quite high. Of course, the level of skill of the potential agent is also a determining factor.

The "zealot" factor must also be considered. A zealot might be, for instance, an individual with a personal motive for revenge so overpowering that it ensures complete dedication to the cause. Or, through intensive training and psychological manipulation, an elite team of fanatic followers can be trained to sacrifice even their own lives to accomplish a given mission. In battle, these trained zealots behave much like the Viking berserker warriors, remaining virtually impervious to injury or pain until either the conflict is resolved or they are forcibly overcome by sheer weight of numbers and loss of blood. When sent out as assassins, such warriors use any covert means available to them to isolate the target and destroy it mysteriously. If captured, which is highly unlikely, they will kill themselves rather than reveal their identity.

One notable example of this kind of warrior is provided by the Japanese kamikaze pilots of World War II, who flung themselves upon the enemy of their people as human bombs, for the sake of *giri*—duty, honor, and glory.

Ninja were once known as the men who could fight or vanish. Using the principle that the enemy could not hit what he did not see, the Ninja devised many methods of getting behind the opponent, thereby forcing him to look over his shoulder to catch sight of the agent. Not many people can fight well in that position. Then, too, an attack from behind is doubly effective since the adversary cannot adequately prepare for it or defend against it.

Furthermore, Ninja are adept at dodging and evading the attacks of the opponent. This ability gives the accomplished Ninja a better than 50 percent chance of successfully avoiding a missile, such as an arrow or thrown dagger. This is true even if the missile is launched from out of sight, which would catch any normal man unawares.

Most Ninja fight better unarmed. Striking with the hands and feet, as well as using throwing and falling techniques, enables the practitioner to initiate multiple attacks or to strike multiple opponents simultaneously. Such open-hand strikes may be sufficient to stun or kill the enemy with a single blow, unless he is of exceptional stature.

Ninja at this level train almost constantly, honing their reflexes, "sharpening their tools," forging their bodies in the fire of their will. They are the epitome of the Ninja legends, believing that nothing is impossible. They are beyond the stage of competition with other martial artists. Instead, each Ninja plays against himself, the only adversary worthy of contention.

ONE MUST KEEP SILENT

The concept of "silence" in ninjitsu is not meant to imply secrecy, or reticence to share information on any level. Rather, it conveys the lack of necessity for comment. Those who know do not need to be told; and those who do not know seldom listen.

Prolonged study of esoteric forces along with practicing the exercises that develop conscious control of the energy centers of the body bring concurrently a subconscious knowledge and intuitive understanding of the forces of Nature. This enables the Ninja to develop certain powers that are latent in all humans.

First, due to self-knowledge and confidence, the Ninja

is resistant to all forms of flattery, suggestion, and intimidation. The ability to mask his mind against interrogation and conceal the true motive of an assignment evolves simultaneously, thus lending an implacable air of calmness to the Ninja's demeanor.

Second, by controlling his body, the Ninja can induce states of diminished respiration and heart rate sufficient to simulate death. This is the power of suspended animation of the Hindu masters. With this, the Ninja acquires the skill of healing wounds by meditative means alone, if need be.

These first two powers lead to acquiring the power of empathy, not only with other people, but also with pets and wild animals. Some Ninja report a certain rapport even with plants. This enables the practitioner to move in harmony with Nature, thus rendering him invisible for all practical purposes.

In the final stages, the Ninja learns to direct the energy of the earth and influence change in accordance with his will. This is the level of the "Vibrating Palm," in which the mere wave of a hand may be sufficient to cause death, either instantly or on a delayed basis. This is the foundation of the *dim mak* or "death touch."

With an understanding of the cosmic forces, the Ninja automatically gains an air of calm dignity. Any need to prove himself in battle is long past, as is any trepidation accompanying the initiation into the art of love by a member of the opposite sex. Until that initiation, the mysteries of the universe remain concealed behind an almost mystical veil. Thereafter it becomes apparent that every being possesses all the latent elements of sexuality, in one form or another. This is seen as *Yang* and *Yin*. Yang is positive, masculine, and white, representing the right side and a force from above; and Yin is negative, feminine, and black, representing the left side and rising from below. Yang could also be described as "power," restless and in perpetual pursuit; and Yin as "love," passive and enveloping. Yin is ever circling Yang, which is always striving to move forward. From this action is formed the whirling staircase of the universe.

Each individual carries both aspects, Yin and Yang, positive and negative, within the self. When the electric energy dominates, the person is said to be more masculine; when the magnetic holds sway, the person is said to be more feminine. Few are capable of complete balance. Therefore people tend to seek, or fall prey to, an energy that is complementary. This is the meaning of the phrase "water seeks its own level" and provides the foundation for virtually all interaction between humans.

2.
The
Nei Ching

Before presenting the mind-control exercises of the Ninja, it is important to have some idea why they work. Therefore I have started this section of the book with excerpts from the *Nei Ching*, the world's oldest known book on medicine. This begins with the *Su Wen,* a transcript of conversations between Huang Ti, the Yellow Emperor of China circa B.C. 3000, and Ch'i Po, his master physician.

I have heard that in ancient times, the people lived to be over one hundred years old, and yet remained active and did not become decrepit in their activities. But in our time, they only reach half that age and become weak and failing. Is it that mankind is degenerating through the ages and is losing his original vigor and vitality?

In ancient times, the people understood the Tao, the great principle of the universe. They patterned themselves upon the laws of Yin and Yang, were sober and led regular simple lives in harmony with Nature. For these reasons, they were healthy in mind and body, and could live to a ripe old age. In our time, they drink alcohol as if it were water, seek all manner of physical pleasure and abandon themselves to intemperance. Their passions exhaust their vital forces, their cravings dissipate their

true essence, they do not know how to find con-
tentment within themselves. They are not skilled in
the control of their spirits and devote all their
attention to the amusement of the mind. For these
reasons they degenerate and do not live beyond the
age of fifty. The sage teaches us to lead a simple
and peaceful life; keeping energy in reserve prevents attack by illness; guarding against desires, the
heart will be at peace; so while the body may
fatigue, the mind does not. In this way one may
still reach the age of one hundred.

Yin in the interior is the guardian of Yang; Yang
in the exterior motivates Yin. Yin and Yang are the
Tao of heaven and earth (the laws of unity and
opposition), the fundamental principle of the ten
thousand things (which creates all matter and its
transmutations), the originators of change, the
beginning of birth (creation) and death (the
destruction of all things), and the storehouse of
all that is mysterious in the natural world. . . .
The treatment and prevention of disease must be
sought in this basic law.

Now the Yin and Yang have name, but no form.
Thus they can be extended from one to ten, ten
to a hundred, one hundred to a thousand, then
to ten thousand, so that they include all things.
All things may be classified according to their
nature.

When speaking of Yin and Yang, the exterior is
Yang, the interior Yin; when speaking of the body,
the back is Yang, the abdomen Yin; when speaking
of the solid and hollow organs, the liver, heart,
spleen, lungs, and kidney are solid and Yin; the gall
bladder, stomach, large intestine, small intestine,
[and] bladder . . . are all hollow and Yang. Thus,
the back is Yang and the Yang within the Yang is
the heart; the Yin within the Yang is the lungs. The
abdomen is Yin and the Yin within the Yin is the
kidneys; the Yang within the abdomen is the liver

and the spleen.

Yin and Yang wax and wane. Functional movement belongs to Yang, which is electric, while nourishing substances are Yin, or magnetic; nor can one exist without the other. Thus are the myriad things able to come to birth. Yin and Yang acting upon one another, producing change.

In acupuncture, there is a facet of treatment known as "obtaining chi," whereby the physician determines if the point selected for treatment is applicable and appropriate for the patient. This may be done by slightly irritating the point, or by pinching gently. In either event, if the proper reaction occurs, that is the site of treatment. The method relies on the circulation of energy in the meridians of the body to be effective.

The *Nei Ching* says, "Man possesses four seas and twelve meridians, which are like rivers that flow to the ocean" (Figure 1). The Sea of Nourishment represents the stomach. If there is too much energy, there is swelling of the abdomen; too little, and the patient cannot eat. The Sea of Blood is the meeting point of the twelve rivers. When there is excess, one feels heavy; when there is a deficiency, one feels uneasy. The Sea of Energy passes through the Gate of Jade, at the base of the skull; when it is affected, one feels pain in the chest, presents a flushed expression, and has a sensation of breathlessness; when there is not enough energy, one cannot speak. Last is the Sea of Marrow. When it is overfull, one experiences an excess of energy; when it is empty, one experiences dizzy spells, tinnitus, pain in the calf muscle, and fainting.

Likewise, each organ stores the vital energy (except for those that transform and transport it). From these reservoirs, the Ninja may draw sufficient power, in the form of chi, to perform his will. This requires an understanding of the nature of energy, as well as knowledge of how it circulates in the body. In the demonstration of *tameshiwara,* the breaking of bricks or stones with the bare hand, the chi forms a protective glove that prevents serious injury.

The means whereby chi may be summoned are few. All

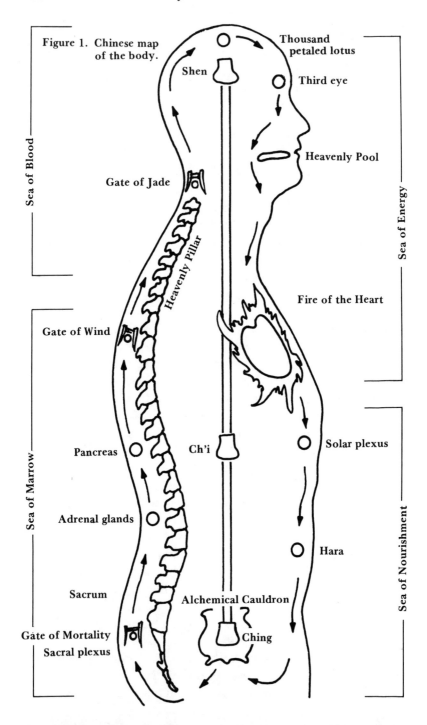

Figure 1. Chinese map of the body.

Thousand petaled lotus
Shen
Third eye
Heavenly Pool
Gate of Jade
Heavenly Pillar
Fire of the Heart
Gate of Wind
Pancreas
Ch'i
Solar plexus
Adrenal glands
Hara
Sacrum
Alchemical Cauldron
Gate of Mortality
Sacral plexus
Ching

Sea of Blood
Sea of Marrow
Sea of Energy
Sea of Nourishment

obey the laws of acupuncture. It should be mentioned that one cannot truly direct the energy of the body; rather, by study and practice it is possible to establish a certain harmony, to become attuned, which makes it possible to attain the higher levels of consciousness. Then and only then, if it is necessary, can one see the mysteries. If one knows what to do and how to do it, one can make the impossible seem commonplace.

3.
Chi Kung: Breathing Exercises

Essentially, *chi kung* is the art of breath control. Inhaling fresh air, one saturates the blood with oxygen. Through the device of mental imagery, which results in unconscious tensing of the appropriate muscles, the "charged" blood arrives at the designated site, promoting the general health and well-being of the selected tissue. Even more profound effects are possible when one is operating on a hormonal level, and beyond that, on the psychic level. This is an art of self-revelation, which is self-regulating and mysterious.

All of the chi kung and *kuji-kiri* techniques presented are methods of directing the flow of energy within the body to specific areas, organs, or points. These techniques are derived from the ancient yogic and tantric traditions that predate recognized civilization. Each posture is designed to act on the body in a precise manner to improve the circulation: They can be used to maintain good health, heal injuries, and cure disease.

WARNING: The exercises demonstrated in this and the next chapter are profound and powerful in the extreme, and the reader is most earnestly warned and cautioned not to attempt any of these movements without first consulting his or her physician. The channeling of vital life-force in the body is not to be taken lightly. These meditation techniques are the foundation of the art of ninjitsu. They should not be

performed in excess, or to the point of fatigue. Do not over-
exert yourself. A Ninja never strains.

COLLECTING THE CHI

Having achieved the first level of skill in the development
of psychic abilities, i.e., the cultivation of and recognition of
the energy source we refer to as chi, it next becomes necessary to practice the collection and transmission of this force.

Filling the hara with chi is the first step. The Chinese
classics refer to inhaling, drawing the air deep into the *hara,*
then holding the breath for extended periods while imagining the circulation of energy within the body. Take care in
practicing this method, since you may rupture the small vessels in the neck and face by improperly trying to retain the
breath. Likewise, don't inhale as much as you can and expect
to keep it all. Let out about half the inhalation; this is easier
to hold and more relaxing to the body. Count your heartbeats at first; after a while, it will not be necessary. Practice
twice a day.

At first it will be difficult to sit still for long. The legs will
ache or fall asleep from lack of circulation. The hands may
tingle or the palms itch. If this happens, fold the fingers
around the thumbs to prevent the chi from flowing out
through them. It is best to practice in a quiet place, but even
then a leaf may fall. When these things are no longer distract-
ing, merely noticed objectively, you have reached the level
known as "tranquillity." That is to say, even sudden noises
do not startle you. At that point you may hear a ringing in
the ears, soft whistles, or whispers; you may see flashes of
light or geometric patterns. All of these have meaning to the
seeker and manifest upon the universal plane of symbolism.
Thus they are known to all, but not all know them.

A word must be spoken about the concentration and
repeated emphasis on breathing and breath control. Respiration is the link between the conscious and subconscious
minds. It is one of the few physical responses over which
everyone has power. All the others—walking, control of the
organs of digestion and elimination, not belching in public—

must be learned. But everyone can hold his breath on command; even infants do it instinctively when dropped into pools of water to learn swimming.

Further, respiration rates often indicate mood. Rapid and shallow breathing indicates fear, deep and slow breathing suggests sleep. Conversely, altering the respiration rate alters the mood. By concentrating on relaxation and relaxing images, the student can program a calmer personality.

The concept of chi may seem mysterious to the Westerner. The idea that some sort of psychic nourishment could be obtained from the air seems farfetched until one remembers that the ancients had no way of describing the differences among nitrogen, oxygen, and carbon dioxide. They simply understood that air contained the "vital life force," because when breathing stopped, so did life.

By focusing attention on breathing, the autonomic and conscious nervous systems establish a rapport together, much like two dancers, and the mind and body are in harmony. With practice, a high degree of control over the body can be achieved. Likewise, this leads to an understanding of oneself, and a calmness and inner peace in one's daily life. If one learns nothing else, this power of relaxation is worth the time required to develop it. That itself leads one to all the other questions and answers.

4.
Kuji-Kiri: The Nine Levels of Power

The Japanese have a name for the finger-knitting exercise of the Ninja. It is called *kuji-kiri,* or literally, the "nine cuts." In the Hindu and Tibetan traditions, they are called *mudras.* It is believed that when one reaches a certain level of training, the hands automatically form the fingerlocks in times of contemplation or stress. Some schools add chants or *mantras;* others vigorously rub beads between their hands. Regardless, the hands are regarded as a microcosm of the body, so to stimulate or sedate the flow of energy and blood therein is certain to have an effect, even a mild or moderate one, upon the rest of the system.

By associating specific meanings and symbols to each of these interlocking patterns, the Ninja were able to program themselves to withstand any torture or accomplish any feat. This gave rise to the legends of their superhuman prowess. And while the finger patterns had an effect on the user, because the knowledge of the connections of the hands to the body are known to everyone, albeit on a subconscious level in most cases, the patterns also had an effect on the audience. Thus, kuji-kiri is the Ninja art of influencing the minds of others with unconscious gestures. When properly performed, the subject is totally unaware of being manipulated.

Certain extrasensory perception (ESP) tests involve the

transmission of rudimentary images from one mind to another. This, of course, is only possible with visually oriented
subjects. Additionally, the symbols used must be those found
in antiquity that have meaning for all on a subconscious level,
and which are thereby easily recognizable even to the uninitiated. Furthermore, certain gestures are unconsciously
received and recognized.

The hands have always been of tremendous significance in
Chinese cosmology, representing a microcosm of the elemental relationships of the universe. Placing the open palms together before the chest is a symbol of peace or prayer. A fist
symbolizes aggression or anger. In ninjitsu, the open left palm
covering the closed right fist is known as the Sign of Eternity,
and means "hidden knowledge." The connections, or circuits,
formed by the finger-knitting exercises serve to circulate the
energy along prescribed pathways within the body.

Some years ago, in a motion picture called *The Last Ninja,*
there was a scene in which a government representative was
trying to encourage a Ninja agent to become involved in an
assignment. When the camera looked over the Ninja's shoulder so we could see what the other man was saying, the Ninja
performed kuji-kiri by rubbing his fingertips with his thumb,
the sign for money. When shown from the government man's
perspective, the agent's hands appeared to be resting, not
moving at all.

The manipulation involved here is so subtle that it appears
to be invisible, so profound that it works every time; therefore the victim is helpless before it. In fact, many principles
of modern-day advertising rely on the same subtle cues and
control of the subject's mind. Because the uninitiated have
no chance against a master of this art, the skill of kuji-kiri
is not taught outside the inner circle of adepts. It is taught
only to those who have mastered themselves so as to be
devoid of selfish motives, and who are therefore unlikely to
use the Way of the Nine Cuts for unscrupulous purposes.

THE NINE LEVELS

In Chinese medicine, the body is divided into three

regions: the upper, middle, and lower. The upper refers to the region above the diaphragm; the middle refers to the area between the upper and the navel; and the lower refers to everything below the navel, including the legs. This trio is traditionally used to designate the internal organs of the body. The topmost section includes the heart and lungs; the middle includes the liver, spleen, and stomach; while the lower includes the bladder, kidneys, and the small and large intestines. In Western terms, the three regions refer to the thoracic, abdominal, and pelvic cavities.

Where the Chinese speak of three regions, the Ninja define *nine* levels of power. This is because each of the three levels also generates an electromagnetic field or "aura," and each of these generates an accompanying specific frequency of vibrational energy, giving a total of nine. To harmonize these various components is the goal of meditation.

In ninjitsu it is taught that one must know the nine levels of power. These are contained and represented in the finger-knitting positions of the kuji-kiri practice. Details of the characteristics and attributes of each position are given in another work, *Secrets of the Ninja*. Here they are presented as taught in the Japanese system, as one complete set of movements, flowing from first to last rhythmically, in conjunction with breath control. They are derived from the Tibetan lama chanting practice, whereby one may attain enlightenment. These are the oldest exercises of this type, and have survived from prehistoric times.

The nine levels of power are as follows:

1. *Rin*—"Strength" of mind and body; in Chinese, *chu;*
2. *Kyo*—"Direction of energy"; in Chinese, *shen;*
3. *Toh*—"Harmony" with the universe; in Chinese, *tai;*
4. *Sha*—"Healing" of self and others; in Chinese, *sha;*
5. *Kai*—"Premonition" of danger; in Chinese, *kai;*
6. *Jin*—"Knowing the thoughts of others"; in Chinese, *jen;*

7. *Retsu*—"Mastery of time and space"; in Chinese, *tung;*

8. *Zai*—"Control" of the elements of nature; in Chinese, *hua;*

9. *Zen*—"Enlightenment"; in Chinese, *tao.*

The kuji-kiri positions that embody the nine levels of power are used as a mnemonic device to train the Ninja both mentally and physically. The progression of movements from one to another symbolizes the movements of the chi within the body.

When one is only beginning to learn, however, each level of energy and power is contemplated in turn during individual sessions so that one may fully explore the potential of each. Then, after much practice, they may be strung together as a mystical in-sign, or occult salute, between members of the same ryu.

1. STRENGTH

The first finger-knitting position of the mystic kuji-kiri salute has the fingers interlocked outside, with the middle fingers, representing the fire element, extended with their tips touching (Figure 2). While exhaling, concentrate the gaze on the point where you feel a pulse. This *kanji,* or mudra, is the symbol for strength of mind and body. It is said that to be a Ninja, one must first be strong, then know, then dare, then be silent. The *Tao Te Ching* says, "Work is done, then forgotten; thus, it lasts forever." One endures, not taking credit, doing what must be done. This is known as inner strength. This posture is not based on hoping for a better afterlife or incarnation, doing penance for past deeds, or preparing for future possible difficulties. Rather, it is concerned with the spirituality of daily activity. To accomplish this, one must wait, and take pleasure in the waiting.

Figure 2.

2. DIRECTION OF ENERGY

Extending the index fingers and curling the corresponding middle finger around each while keeping the other fingers interlocked forms the second kanji (Figure 3). This represents the ability to direct the flow of energy within the body. The first posture develops the student's sensory withdrawal skills, making one aware of the internal sounds and vibrations. In time, the power to harmonize with this flow of internal energy enables one to develop psychokinetic abilities. The finger entwining is similar to, and symbolic of, the two serpents on the medical caduceus. In fact, the caduceus may have been the source from which this kanji was derived. In Hindu hatha yoga, as well, there are two intertwining channels of energy that unite the various centers of power within the body.

Figure 3.

3. HARMONY

When one understands the concept and principles of meditation, all differences between oneself and the object of concentration disintegrate and one develops an awareness of the universe. Good health flows naturally to the practitioner. The finger position here represents the fire element. One begins to follow the proper path instinctively, with the hands automatically forming the correct linkage, or kanji (Figure 4). At this stage, an appreciation of all life becomes manifest. Animals can sense this inner peace, making it seem that the practitioner can almost speak with them. One could walk safely through a pit full of serpents without coming to harm, since the animals can recognize this presence. This is analogous to a bee-keeper mentally picturing a hexagon, which sets up a harmonic vibration throughout his person that the insects consider nonthreatening.

Figure 4.

4. HEALING

The power to kill and restore life is symbolized by the finger-knitting position in which the index fingers are extended, with the other fingers interlocked (Figure 5). One who displays this gesture understands the energies of the body and can direct them to heal injuries and cure disease, within both himself and others. In the latter case, the practitioner does not transmit energy to the patient; instead, he generates the patient's own energy, then directs it to the appropriate site. Thus in its positive aspect this kanji confers great healing ability; conversely, it also confers the power to take life as well. All of the vital points of the body and the internal organs are made vulnerable by this exercise. Feel the pulse between the fingertips in this position. The source of power for this skill is the solar plexus.

Figure 5.

5. PREMONITION

The hand-clasping gesture of this kanji reassures and calms the mind (Figure 6). Merchants often rub their hands together before a negotiation, to relax themselves and in anticipation. Shiatsu, the art of acupressure, also advocates warming the hands by rubbing them before touching a patient, so as not to shock him or her. Place the palms together and interlace the fingers from above. Not only does this movement serve to calm oneself in times of danger, it also is the key to developing the sixth sense that permits the premonition of danger. Users of this ability can feel the emotions of those around them, and often develop sensitivity to psychic impressions. Further, it conveys to the practitioner certain powers over his physical body, including suspended animation and the power to withstand extremes of heat and cold.

Figure 6.

6. KNOWING THE THOUGHTS OF OTHERS

Point the fingertips down and interlace them. Then fold the palms down over the fingers by lowering the elbows and cross the thumbs (Figure 7). This gesture represents inner knowledge, signifying that the practitioner has the power to read the thoughts of others. It signifies further that the validity of the mental impression may be confirmed by other secret tests. This is the *Saimenjitsu* ("Way of the Mind Gate") symbol for telepathy, which also permits nonverbal communication with other like-minded individuals. Concurrent with this ability, one also learns to form a mental barrier against the thoughts of others, and to project an impresssion that is false. This is called "masking the intention." Persons skilled in this art make excellent negotiators and are capable of great empathy and compassion. Exhale while focusing on this hand position. Concentrate on listening to the inner voice.

Figure 7.

Figure 8.

7. MASTERY OF TIME AND SPACE

This finger-knitting mudra is formed by curling the fingers of the right hand around the extended index finger of the clenched left hand, and pressing against the outside edge of the fingernail with the right thumb (Figure 8). In acupuncture, this point is known as *Sho Yo,* the "Young Merchant" point. Used in the treatment of fever and diarrhea, the method is to press inward strongly with a sharp object, while inhaling for nine heartbeats (seven to ten seconds), and to do this three times. In meditation one need only touch this point, the large intestine meridian point number one, to remember it. This gesture imparts mastery of time and space at a range of three to five feet, depending on the student's level of accomplishment. It is related to the third eye, and can be employed to freeze an opponent psychically, much as the *kiai* does with sound. With multiple opponents, a sufficiently baleful stare can intimidate them long enough to permit an escape. It can be used then to suspend or hold time in proportion to one's degree of concentration. In advanced stages, it can be set to block a doorway, prevent pursuit, or slow the action of poison or fire.

Figure 9.

8. CONTROL

This kanji represents control of the elements of Nature. In this case, it would be more accurate to say that it is a state in which one perceives the way of Nature and elects to act in harmony with it, rather than to imply that one bends the elements to one's will, which, of course, is quite impossible. The gesture itself (Figure 9) is symbolic of the "Thousand-Petaled Lotus," the actual cortical surface of the brain. It symbolizes the physiological aspects that arise when hormone-enriched blood, full of the endorphins chemically produced by the body as a result of the meditation exercises, suddenly flood over the brain, bringing a sense of oneness and profound well-being. Although the ancient physicians had no way of adequately describing such an anatomical phenomenon to their students, their intuitive concept is quite accurate in all respects. Obviously, such an experience cannot be adequately described by mere words. Therefore, little more can be explained regarding this kuji-kiri technique. At this stage one attains true invisibility. Acting in harmony with all, there is no contention.

9. ENLIGHTENMENT

The Hidden-Hand gesture (Figure 10) indicates that the
initiate has attained *satori,* nirvana, or ultimate bliss. Which-
ever name is used, the meaning is clear: final understanding
of oneself and others. Having passed through the pillars of
self-doubt, and looked long and deeply into the mirror of
self-knowledge, one comes to know oneself. One ceases
regretting and blaming the past for current misfortunes;
one stops awaiting the coming of a better tomorrow; one
is able to be here now, to enjoy each bite of food at the meal.
This lesson can only be learned by those who have been
hungry. To stare in awe at the sunrise, marveling at the intri-
cacy of life itself upon this planet—this is known as following
the middle way. Those who present this gesture and know its
true meaning are often known as teachers.

Figure 10.

SUMMARY OF THE STEPS IN
LEARNING KUJI-KIRI

1. *Sensory withdrawal*—sitting alone in a comfortable position in a quiet place.
2. *Relaxation response*—elicited by fixing attention on breathing.
3. *Sensitivity to psychic impressions*—from cultivating and collecting chi within the body.
4. *Circulation of energy*—having awareness of the ebb and flow of energy in Nature and the ability to move with it.
5. *Balance*—internal rapport; physical and mental equilibrium that brings with it understanding of self and others.
6. *Harmony*—external rapport; the power to absorb and reflect energy from other sources in such a way that, when you prevail, the opponent opens his heart to you and becomes an equal; thus all conflict vanishes.
7. *Application*—learning to do anything by doing it; the key is practice, then patience and perseverance. Setting realistic goals and seeing things clearly; sharing your knowledge with other seekers.

EXPERIENCING CHI IN BATTLE

We have spoken before of how energy circulates in the body. Most students have found the following an adequate description of the sensations of chi in combat.

First, the hara feels warm. The chi ascends the spine, making it feel as if covered with armor. The feet are rooted to the ground, no matter what the surface, and one feels solidly planted, i.e., balanced and poised, yet not tense. If there is any tension in the front of the body, it is felt mildly in the hara and along the insides of the legs. In most instances, the hands are raised defensively in front of the chest. In ninjitsu, one feels the chi being directed forward as a sphere of energy, capable of absorbing and reflecting any attack from whatever quarter. Head and eyes seem detached, seeing everything at once, as if not part of the conflict at all. The mind is calm, expecting nothing and reacting instantly.

This is the state known as "no-mind" in the writing of Musashi, the famous Zen swordsman, who survived over sixty duels in feudal Japan and died peacefully in his bed.

Having accomplished this, one must apply it to proper movement. In olden times it was said one must already be a *yudansha* (black belt) to study ninjitsu. That is because at this level, one must return to one's original teachings and apply the principles of movement to them. All martial arts teach meditation on the hara, but few know why. It is because, for proper movement, the *waist must move first.* One could learn any style or system and miss this important lesson. Having learned it, however, one returns to the practice forms with renewed interest and enthusiasm. Thus there is nothing new to learn, only further understanding.

5.
The Five
Elements

In order to become a warrior-mystic, the student must fill his body with the chi energy he has collected and cultivated in the hara. The classics refer to the hara as the "Golden Stove" in which the various elements of alchemical magic are blended together into the elixir of immortality.

The primary attribute of the warrior is strength; that of the mystic is intelligence. The combination of these two produces the Ninja, who draws upon his occult powers to develop his strategy, and upon his understanding of the way of Nature to choose his tactics.

The Ninja seldom wear armor, since to do so implies the existence of an external threat as well as a willingness to engage in battle. Instead they practice in private, making no show, developing their balance and martial ability concurrently with both mental and physical exercises. In the beginning, many Ninja keep notes, fostering the belief in sacred scrolls and tori-maki. But eventually the mind becomes developed to the extent that memorization is not only possible but preferred. Then too, as understanding becomes greater, less and less structures and thought forms are required; lists and long litanies of creed are relied on much less.

In the previous section, it was indicated that each finger represents an element. In this section, we will go further and demonstrate how each also represents an organ. The progressive elevation of energy symbolized by the successive finger-knitting positions acts to channel healing, oxygen-enriched blood through the body in accordance with the laws of the five elements. This serves to maintain the health and well-being of the Ninja as well as to teach the secrets of the universe.

Each of the fingers is associated with a specific organ of the body by virtue of the network of nerves, blood vessels, acupuncture meridians, and psychic channels. Likewise each organ is representative of one of the five primary elements, air, water, earth, fire, and wood (void). The old texts say that this is because there are five elements and five fingers; it makes perfect sense, in light of ancient logic. Even if all the fingers are not present, as in the case of the Yakuza (Japanese gamblers), who sometimes cut off parts of their fingers in a ritual of "token suicide" for a debt they cannot pay, the energy shell remains continuous. That is, as circulation is restored to an area of injury, along with it comes chi, which pervades and passes through all things and is found in abundance everywhere.

You should understand that the symbolism of gestures and the mental direction of energy is far more important than the physical act of connecting various circuits, although the gestures do tend to reinforce the practice and act as significant triggers for physiological and psychological responses. Just as Pavlov's dogs salivated at the sound of a bell, so too can man program himself for whatever purpose is desired.

The elements are each represented by an exercise or special breathing technique designed either to tone up or sedate a particular type of energy within the body. These are called the Five Elements Exercises. Two require moving, two are static, and the last is a combination of both.

The *Nei Ching* says: "The five elements—wood, fire, earth, air, and water—encompass all the phenomena of Nature. It is a symbolism that applies itself equally to man." Just as things may be classified according to their Yin and Yang aspects, they may be further divided into their elemental components. These interact in specific and prescribed manners, the alteration of which is not possible and the study of which may consume a lifetime.

The *Nei Ching* says further:

> Fire creates earth (ash), which creates air (smoke), which creates water (condensation), which creates wood (life), which creates fire (energy). This is the cycle of creation. Wood destroys earth (by covering), fire destroys air (by combustion), earth destroys water (by retention), air destroys wood (by smothering), water destroys fire (by extinguishing). This is the cycle of destruction, the Yin and Yang of Nature, the inevitable law of change [Figure 11].

If there is excess energy in an organ, it may be dissipated at the point of sedation for that organ. The organ which follows in the circulation of energy will then receive the excess energy and the

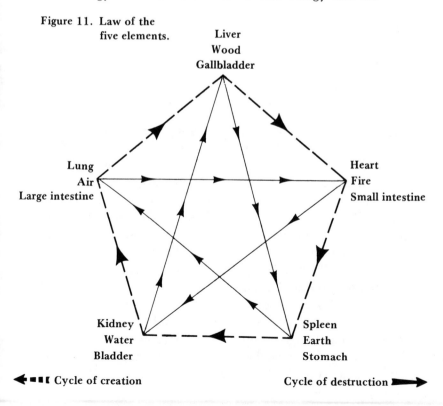

Figure 11. Law of the five elements.

Liver
Wood
Gallbladder

Lung
Air
Large intestine

Heart
Fire
Small intestine

Kidney
Water
Bladder

Spleen
Earth
Stomach

◄ ∎∎⦗ Cycle of creation

Cycle of destruction ∎∎►

preceding one will be sedated. Therefore the sedation point for one organ is the point of tonification for the next one in sequence.

Each organ meridian is also possessed of a master point known as the source; a *lo* point, which acts on coupled organs; a connecting point with other meridians; an approval point on the bladder meridian; an alarm point on the abdomen; an ancient control point; and a point that is forbidden.

EARTH

Interlock the fingers, keeping the tips of the thumbs touching; exhale and empty the lungs, tensing the hara (Figure 12). The earth element is related to the spleen. It is the center of the physical and spiritual body. When concentrating on this level, one will experience sensations of taste and feel. Worry injures the spleen, which governs the liver in the circulation of energy; sitting too long is also a strain.

Inhale deeply and fully, filling the lungs from bottom to top, as if pouring water into a glass. Imagine the vital energy (prana, chi) of the air being drawn deeply into the body, filling it with energy. Lift the hands with fingers laced up to throat level (Figure 13). If you wish, mentally repeat, "In comes the good air." Turn the hands over and push upward above the head as you exhale. Recite, "Out goes the bad air," removing all impurities and poisons. Hold this position, then lower the hands to the top of the head, thinking, "Enter the healing white light." Exhale, returning the hands to the lap. Repeat this exercise nine times.

Figure 12.

Figure 13.

Figure 14.

WATER

Begin with the hands resting lightly on the knees. Let the hands float upward as if suspended from the wrists, inhaling deeply as before (Figure 14). Then exhale, emptying the lungs fully, as the hands lower slowly once again (Figure 15). Repeat nine times. This encourages oxygen-saturated blood to be pumped to the kidneys, representing the water element, which heals and stimulates the power of the will. Water is the symbol of love; and fear as well as standing overly long are injurious. When utilizing this type of energy, one experiences hearing sensations, sometimes known as the "music of the spheres." This technique maintains and invigorates the anti-specific immune system of the body. Do not overdo it. If one is ill or has allergies, this exercise is of great benefit.

Figure 15.

AIR

The air element is represented by the lungs and the large intestine. In hatha yoga, the finger position shown here is used to press against the acupuncture point that invigorates the large intestine. This exercise does likewise. With hands resting on the lap, in the position shown (Figure 16), breathe deeply and silently, in and out through the nose, and imagine that the energy is circulating up the back and down the front of the body. Repeat this exercise seven times. This calms the mind and improves the digestion. It also stimulates the chi, or vital energy of the body. Lying down too much is injurious to this organ. The lungs are the Yin, or empty, side; while the colon is the Yang, or full side.

Figure 16.

FIRE

The heart represents the fire element. This is the site of all psychic energy. With fingertips almost touching, raise the arms in a circle as shown (Figure 17). Inhale, imagining the energy entering the right fingers, passing through the heart, and exiting out through the fingers of the left hand as you exhale. Repeat three times. The physiological symbolism here is of the abdominal aorta and the ascending aorta.

Figure 17.

WOOD

The liver is the body's expression of the wood element. Remember, earth and fire are linear; water and air are circular in nature; and wood, or the void as it is sometimes known, symbolizes circular growth about a linear axis, thus uniting the two types of energy.

Inhale, lifting the arms out to the sides, with palms down, then up above the head. Now exhale, pulling down an imaginary pillar directly in front of the body's centerline (Figure 18). Stop at throat level, holding without strain one half of the full breath. Look between the hands and imagine you are holding a ball of energy. After a while, you will feel a tingling in the palms. Later, you may begin to see the energy itself. Repeat this exercise nine times.

Wood is related to the planet Jupiter, known even in ancient times and highly regarded in alchemical circles. It is the source of the spirit and the seat of the higher self. This energy may be used for whatever purposes the practitioner desires, for by the time this level is achieved, all thoughts of self and personal gain have been put aside. The liver is related to the eyes; thus, it is often said that those with this power have flashing eyes or can kill with a look. The Tiger style of kung fu, based on the wood element, may lead its students to visual sensations. One must have great strength of will not to fall prey to hallucinations at this level.

Figure 18.

6.
Nei Kung: Internal Strength

Prolonged practice of the internal exercises shown here enables the practitioner to gain some degree of control over his or her physical being. When this is accomplished, the *genin,* or lower self, is quieted and calmed, which permits liberation of the higher levels of being. Interestingly, the term *genin* is also applied to the field agent in ninjitsu, indicating to the higher ranks *(chunin* and *jonin)* that he is not above the third level of comprehension, and so is concerned with survival and conquest rather than peace and harmony.

Control of the body leads to control of the mind. When one knows how to control one's mind, the impossible becomes commonplace. To demonstrate this for the edification of others is an expression of ego. There is no need to prove one's power to anyone other than oneself. Those that have it, know it; those who do not can never recognize it. There is no proof of anything; there are only lessons and tests.

CONTROL OF THE BODY

By concentrating on one's breathing, the mind becomes aware of internal sounds. In time this will develop into the ability to withdraw the consciousness from the physical being to the inner sanctum and fortress of the mind. In such a state of meditative balance, the body is sustained and protected by the energized electromagnetic aura which Western science has only recently acknowledged. This permits the user to withstand extremes of heat and cold that are unbearable for the untrained, to breathe underwater, to be buried alive, and to walk through flames unharmed. Fakirs who walk on hot coals or sit on beds of nails are demonstrating this power. Depending on the student's degree of mastery, this state may be maintained for as long as concentration permits.

With more experience, the disciple may develop superior balance, allowing him to adjust the weight of his body by muscular tension. This makes it possible to walk tightwires, climb walls, move silently, and fall without injury. The art of *ukemi* (judo break-falling) is based on this, as well as the technique of expanding or reducing the size of the body. The best example of this was the famous Houdini, who puffed up his chest when being bound with ropes, then relaxed and had sufficient slack to wriggle free of the bonds. Conversely, the Hindu who folds himself into a trunk or jar that appears too small to contain him illustrates reduction. With this mental control, any part of the body can withstand injury without harm and may equally be used as a weapon. These techniques are referred to in ancient texts as the Iron Body styles and require *kime* (focus) and *genshin* (balance).

Naturally, all this requires an expenditure of energy. In China, the ability to work steadily at a task until its completion without food or water is highly valued. Meditation enables one to calm these desires temporarily, but an equal amount of time must be spent replenishing the source. This power makes it possible to suspend all outward appearance of life and not awaken until the time or signal chosen by the practitioner.

TAMIESHIWARA

Tamieshiwara, or the art of breaking, requires the channeling of chi from the organ of generation and storage, along the meridians and pathways of the body, to the part of the fist making impact. In this case, chi is channeled to the edge of the hand. This strike simulates a death-blow to the back of

Figure 19.

Figure 20.

the neck of an enemy who has been thrown facedown. Only sixteen pounds of pressure are required to break the neck/ brick in this manner; but the stone is harder than the bones of the hand. Therefore, the Ninja develop *kime,* or focus of concentration. While pressing down on the enemy's skull with the left hand to set the vertebrae (Figure 19), strike down with a sharp blow, using the sword hand (Figure 20). Concentrate on driving through the target; you must *want* to injure the brick. This anger injures the spleen, so the practitioner must take care not to use it too often.

DRAGON CLAW

The Dragon Claw technique is a powerful gripping attack that requires great finger strength. This strength is only acquired after ten years of carrying heavy jars by the mouths in each hand. It is characteristic of the Black Dragon ryu. Ripping a telephone book in half is a demonstration of this skill. Using the wrists, twist and snap the spine of the text, breaking it in two (Figures 21 and 22). Gripping the pieces, rip the pages apart in a single shredding tear (Figure 23). One with this ability can knock a man out by squeezing his skull; or rupture him by gripping the rectus abdominus.

Figure 21.

Figure 22.

Figure 23.

7.
Mental
Powers

The Ninja develops his mental powers to a fine art. His powers include mind reading, hypnosis, suggestion, impressment, and other techniques of controlling the outcome of situations.

MIND READING

Everyone has the power to intuit the thoughts of others. Some have developed mind reading to a fine art, while others continue to deny its existence. It is not that we "hear voices," although this is possible; nor that we can transmit and receive symbols visually, the most common ESP test. It means that when we find a beloved family member deeply saddened by a loss, and we seek to comfort that person by touching him or her, at that point we feel a physical sensation of change: we have established a rapport. We can now experience in some small way, the grief or joy of another soul. This feeling of oneness is characteristic of telepathy, or thought transference, and is heightened by emotional stimulation or patient practice.

The goal of mind reading, then, is the establishment of mental rapport with the subject. First, we must determine which type of person we are dealing with: visual, audial, or tactile. Artists are essentially visual, dealing with color, shape, and visual images; musicians exemplify the audial category, concerning themselves with tone, range, and sound; while sculptors might best express the tactile group, working with texture and form. It is interesting to note that touch is the customary test of reality for most people. Seeing an unusual object, they approach cautiously, then reach out to feel if it is there. Likewise an eerie note or whistle emanating from behind a grate will eventually lead the curious to feel for the vibrations at the source of the sound.

The way to determine what type of person we are dealing with is to observe his or her eyes. "The eyes are the windows to the soul." Visual thinkers look up when trying to remember or figure things out; listeners look from side to side (toward the ears); and touchers look down when thinking (Figure 24). Observe to which quadrant the subject glances when thinking. Those who look above the level of the eyes, or appear unfocused, think and remember in pictures. Those who look side to side are listening. Those who glance down and left remember by rote or chant; those who glance down and right are touchers. Looking to the left indicates memory; to the right, reasoning. Holding the forehead (the third eye), rubbing the ears, and stroking the chin are all gestures used to stimulate or encourage mental processes.

Having determined in which category the subject should be placed, we must then adjust ourselves to his or her mode of operation. This is necessary because most people have no idea how they process information; they only know that they do better in some areas than others. When speaking to one who is visually oriented, use words like "see," "get the picture," or "it looks like." This will make it easier for the subject to understand what you are saying and apply it to his own constructs or thought forms. Likewise for listeners, phrases such as "it sounds like," "it has been said," and "I hear what you are saying," are appropriate. For touchers, physical contact is best, but terms like "sensation," "feeling," or "impression" can be applied.

We have now altered ourselves to conform to the framework of the subject, since we cannot hope to alter him. The Ninja knows that to influence the affairs of men, one must be

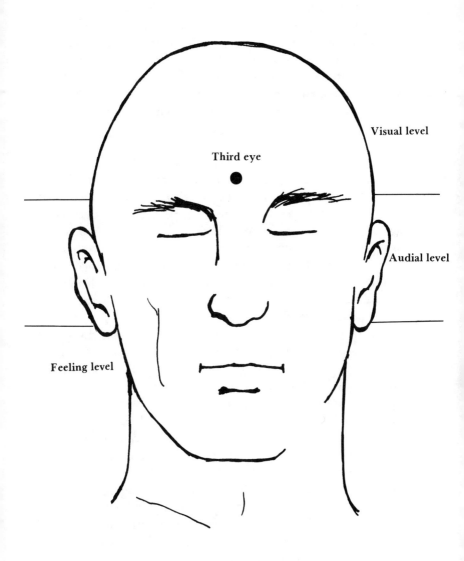

Figure 24. Map of the face.

outside the circle that presses them; we cannot hope to change others until we have control of ourselves.

Another method whereby this may be accomplished, and one that is the most basic form of meditation, is to adjust one's rate of respiration to that of the subject. When experimenting with associates, or practicing techniques together, always begin with this exercise. When the breathing of both parties is synchronized, rapport is achieved. This method may also be used on the unaware subject, since it is so subtle that it goes unnoticed. Nonetheless it is extremely powerful and effective.

Also, synchronizing your body language with that of the subject can increase rapport. For example, you can feel how closely united soldiers on parade are, or church members with their heads bowed in prayer. This must be done carefully, or the subject may accuse you of mocking him derisively.

Once sufficient rapport has been achieved, it then becomes possible to direct the activities of the subject by "leading" him. This is a subtle form of hypnosis, not suitable for stage performance, but adequate for sharing a burden or giving advice. It is impossible to make another person do your bidding by sheer force of will; but if you can get him to follow you, he may accomplish things far beyond any imagined limitations, and you may be permitted to watch, hear, or feel the experience with the subject.

The following is a good test of rapport: When you think you and the subject resonate like tuning forks placed near each other, intentionally begin changing the breathing rate, then the posture, then the tone of the conversation, to a topic of your choosing. If the subject is sad, remind him, in terms he can use, of happier experiences. If he has won a great or even modest victory, rejoice in it with him. Feel the electricity of each moment. Experience the magnetism of charismatic individuals, relive fond memories through the eyes of the elderly, marvel at the wonder of an infant's curiosity.

This is as close as one may come to telepathy, or mind reading. It may be applied with equal facility to negotiation, investigation, or conversation. If one knows how, one can make the impossible seem commonplace.

Although these methods are not readily reproducible in the laboratory, they exist nonetheless. Those who practice soon find how well they work and how powerful they are.

One thing should be noted with regard to reading body language. Whenever an individual makes one of the gestures indicated as a kuji-in position, he or she is unconsciously indicating which state or mood is predominant at that moment. The hands need not be folded together in the elaborate ritual shown here, but anytime one hand covers the other, it indicates hidden knowledge. Whenever the arms, legs, or fingers are crossed, it is a gesture of defense. There are many such "mudras," the study of which may consume a lifetime.

Likewise, if one wishes to set the mood, it is possible to do so subtly by discreetly forming the mudras and not calling attention to them. In this way, they are perceived on a subconscious level. For instance, yawning is a semiconscious gesture, and one easily suggested to a group. Next time you are at a meeting which is exceptionally boring, sit in a comfortable position and yawn. You need not yawn widely; in fact, make it appear that every effort is being made to conceal the yawn out of respect for the speaker. By this or other subtle cues, the rest of the audience can soon be made to doze off. This works well in classrooms, and may be of some value in hostage situations. The more relaxed or even sleepy you appear, the greater the chance that others, even a kidnapper, may either be calmed or made to feel greater stress by having to stay alert. Also, if you, as the hostage, are asleep, you are nonthreatening and that inhibits feelings of hostility on his part. Further, he may pay less attention to guarding you, perhaps providing an opportunity to escape.

HYPNOSIS

The ability to hypnotize others is largely dependent upon their belief that you possess some type of supernatural power. In fact, the Ninja does: he possesses the power to control himself.

Stage hypnotism is a performance in which both the performer and the volunteer subconsciously agree to participate. In this way, the member of the audience becomes a part of the show, fulfilling his hidden desire to share the stage. Only those who are natural leaders and have a good self-image come forward. Nor should the reticent be unduly called or encouraged to take part, since they will become too easily embarrassed and self-conscious.

Basically, the collusion between the players implies that the hypnotist will not injure or insult his assistants while they are onstage with him. If more than one volunteer is employed, most will go along with the gag, since they have their eyes closed, but can still hear the movements of the others as they comply with the simple directions of the performer. He, of course, acts as the director. By having his "actors" follow his "commands," and by informing the audience what they are witnessing, he allows the imagination of each to do most of the work. For the most part, this is the secret of extracorporeal mind control.

The imagined power of the hypnotist has its dark side, as well. After all, if one spends day after day repeatedly manipulating the will of those who step forward at one's beck and call, albeit for simple tasks only, one might come to believe in one's powers, oneself.

SUGGESTION

Suggestion is the ability to plant a seed in the mind of someone else. If the beholder has an active imagination and sufficient motivation, that seed may grow and flourish. This is the basis for many legends of witch doctors "praying a man to death." Conversely, if the listener has sufficient self-confidence and a strong moral code, such seeds of destruction fall on deaf ears, only to wither and die.

A hypochondriac can be made physically ill by repeatedly asking him if he feels well. The supposedly objective feedback requires his participation, since he must answer the question, either aloud or internally. Eventually his mind will fix on some minor ache and magnify its importance until it consumes all his waking thoughts. The imaginary injury will then begin to manifest itself upon the body. This is some-times known as psychosomatic, mind-over-body illness. In Catholicism, there is a history of people manifesting spontaneous bleeding from certain parts of the body. This is known as stigmata.

Of course, good seeds may also be planted and watered with sincerity. If, every day, one is told that he or she is looking fit and trim, whether or not it is true, sooner or later it will begin to sink in. The object of the remarks will actually begin to look and feel better in an unconscious effort to live up to the positive feedback.

Suggestion is a simple and only partially effective technique. To be truly effective, it requires a long period of repetition. That way, the likelihood that the seed will be discredited or cut down is lessened, and it is more likely for the subject to accept the suggestion on his own volition and act on it independently.

IMPRESSMENT

Impressment is a technique for securing the cooperation of someone sympathetic to one's cause. Take, for example, the case of the stage hypnotist who calls for volunteers. Those who volunteer are predisposed to being on stage with the mentalist. Either they would like to catch a glimpse of the hypnotist's power in action, or else they would like to challenge him to overcome them. Even the latter can be induced to comply, however, by a simple mechanism.

Suppose the mentalist has written a prediction on a card and sealed it inside an envelope. He asks for a member of the audience to come up and choose one of several cards from a tray upon which stand several pasteboards, facing the crowd. As the assistant comes behind the table, he sees a note on the back of one of the cards. It reads, "Choose this card for a reward after the show." Or there might be a dollar bill taped to the back to induce him to choose a particular one. In either event, when he has made his choice, miraculously it is the same as the prediction!

Impressment is also used in military basic training. An

individual is chosen from the ranks, either for his exceptional skills or lack of same, and directed to perform for the rest of the platoon. If he has any sense of self-pride, he is obliged to do his best, both by his own self-discipline and by the pressure of his peers, those with whom he must continue to interact. From time to time this method reveals natural leaders.

Also, impressment is a form of discipline used in prison camps, where inmates are obliged to follow orders for fear of punishment or reprisals. In either event, it differs from suggestion in that the former is subliminal, while the latter is a question of choice.

CONTROLLING OPTIONS

This technique involves having the subject appear to make a free decision while actually being made to select the item that is desired. For instance, hold a piece of candy in one hand and nothing in the other. Extend both toward a child and say, "Pick one." If the child selects the fist with the sweet, you may congratulate him or her and present the prize. If, however, the subject chooses the empty hand, then say, "Very well, we eliminate that one, leaving you with the prize!" Again the child "wins," strictly at the whim of the magician.

A similar example can be seen at the breakfast table, when the youngster is asked, "What do you want for breakfast, oatmeal or cereal?" This question implies that the child will eat something, regardless of whether or not he wanted any breakfast in the first place.

Another example is the loaded question, to which no answer is appropriate. When asked, "Have you stopped beating your wife?" if one answers no, it may be understood that one is continuing with the practice. If the answer is yes, then one has confessed to having done the violence previously. If no response is made, the persecutor can claim that the subjet is afraid to respond out of guilt; and if the subject claims a trick question, he can be accused of being overly sensitive or paranoid.

Essentially, this method relies on controlling the options of the subject, so that only one decision, the one desired, is possible, while at the same time, creating the illusion that the subject is free to choose as he pleases.

HYPNOSIS IN COMBAT

In combat, *Hsi men jitsu* ("Way of the Mind Gate"), means the ability to make the enemy do what you want in spite of his own best interests. As previously described, we can make it appear that his self-interest will be served by impressment and so on, but it is also possible to manipulate his behavior by means of trickery.

The late Bruce Lee often spoke of what he called "motor-setting" the opponent in battle. Advance, making a simple attack, and let the enemy parry it. Do this twice. On the third repetition, advance as before, but attack to a different quarter. The enemy, having been programmed by the simple pattern of strike and parry, will observe the advance cue and begin his block a third time. This time, however, the strike is to a different target. According to the creator of *jeet kune do,* this tactic works almost every time.

A simpler version is the classical feint. The Dragon style is a good example of this: If one makes alternating flying and low-sweeping attacks, the enemy, in defending against one, opens himself to the other.

Another effective tactic is to use psychological ploys, such as making the enemy angry by taunting him, thus encouraging him to attack wildly. Feigning injury or helplessness to draw the enemy into range for a strike may be placed in this category, as well. A third, very effective tactic for the Ninja is target denial. By using his evasive abilities, the Ninja avoids the enemy's thrusts and strikes. This, of course, frustrates him.

General Sun Tze has said, "The art of war is based on deception"; it is also based on reflex and misdirection.

8.
Mi Lu Kata: The Lost Track Form

There are very few formal exercises in ninjitsu. This is because it is a science of principles rather than of techniques. Still, the history of an art can be traced through its ritual practices and in the case of ninjitsu, that means the kata.

KATA

Kata, pronounced "gata," is a Japanese word meaning "dance." In ninjitsu this term is applied to a formal set of exercises, performed in proper sequence, demonstrating a specific series of techniques in logical combination. Some kata are historical in nature. That is, they tell a story of some past adventure or some legendary hero. An example of this might be the Hawaiian fire and sword dancers. Some kata are purely for health and self-defense. Still others are technical, and illustrate a specific principle or strategy upon which the various movements are based. An example of this would be *Heian One* of Shotokan karate.

The kata forms are designed to be learned by rote, since man long ago found that that was an effective method of transmitting a complicated body of information from generation to generation. But even when taught in this primitive ritualistic manner, while the fundamental principles and foundations remain intact, each student who learns a kata and then attempts to pass it on must, of necessity, color it with his or her own experience and interpretation. So the art or style evolves and changes, yet remains the same. This is the meaning of the saying: "The way that can be told is not the eternal way." Of course, the more classical the artist, the more exact his forms are, that is, the more successful he is at imitating his instructor, who, it must be hoped, was equally accurate in his own study. Even then, some masters hold back some techniques from poor students. These, also, are lost to the sands of time.

How kata forms came about is an interesting story. During the many "sword-hunt" episodes of the Far East, whether they were Chinese, Japanese, Korean, or Okinawan, unscrupulous rulers tried to disarm their subservient peoples by forbidding them to possess weapons. At first this applied primarily to *katana,* swords; but when the peasants proved themselves still too strong, any device was considered deadly. To this day, knives with blades longer than two inches are forbidden in some districts. Thus the population was reduced to fighting bare handed. And when they became too good at that, boxing was forbidden. Even to practice a martial art was considered insurrection, so secret societies were formed, and training was concealed.

One of the methods by which this was accomplished was kata. By combining the practice movements with the rhythm of music, students could claim they were only dancing, and since they were not striking each other, it was difficult to disprove. In modern times, forms competition accompanied by music is still a popular aspect of tournament play. The tune, melody, and tempo all contribute to the mood, allowing the performer a free rein to flow with the expectations and attention of the crowd.

Emperors and rulers never seem to learn that when repressive measures are implemented, regardless of their justification, the people will tolerate it just so long; then they will find some means of fighting back. Ideas cannot be killed,nor can spirit be crushed. At one time in history, in many parts of the world it was forbidden even to whisper the name of the Silent Way; but it is still here.

IMAGINARY ENEMY

When practicing kata it is important to visualize an opponent. We will discuss later how everyone possesses, in one form or another, certain guides and spirit helpers to aid him or her in the quest for understanding and enlightenment (see Chapter 9). This is true for all. So it is that each also has a secret enemy. It is this individual with whom one "dances" in kata practice.

The fact that many people turn to, or are led to, the martial arts for the purposes of revenge is a sad commentary on mankind's inability to communicate. With time, which heals all wounds, most people learn to overcome this desire and become better men for the experience. This normally occurs just as they become highly competent fighters, capable of extracting whatever retribution they desire. Thus it may be said that the martial arts turn cowards into heroes and bullies into gentlemen.

Until that moment of enlightenment, however, one must cope with the need to "get even" or "mete out justice." The Sage has taught that such feelings of anger may be diverted to energy; and since it is a powerful force, difficult to deny, it should not be wasted. Therefore, in kata we fight an imaginary enemy.

At the beginning of many forms, the performer is asked to stand for a moment and compose himself before beginning the exercise. When training, extend this interval and imagine your deadliest enemy within arm's reach. Practice every move as if defending against him. If your powers of visualization are not adequately developed, listen for the sound of his heartbeat. When properly executed, kata can lead to the real sensation of touch, and evoke the mood of the warrior when he fights. All this is part of the kata. The imagery enhances every aspect of form practice, making it not only more enjoyable for the student, but also more entertaining for those who may be watching. Know also that whenever you bow and start your dance, someone *is* watching. Therefore you must always do your best, if not for applause, at least for the sake of living up to your own standards.

There are very specific techniques for invoking your imaginary enemy. Before beginning kata, sit for a moment in *seiza* (kneeling posture). Think hard and mentally repeat a selected "trigger" word. This word must be chosen carefully so as not to evoke any negative imagery in normal daily existence. One would not choose a common word, for instance; nor would it be wise to choose something overly complicated. It may simply be the enemy's name, or just "enemy," or "kill." Tense your muscles as if preparing to fight. Mentally replay the incident that threatens your self-image as many times as necessary. Let your anger build, feel the pulse in your temple, the heat on your cheeks. When you stand, imagine your enemy in front of you watching, mocking you. Show him!

Perform the exercise with force and power. Visualize the destruction and impact of every punch and kick. Put emotional content into each movement. When you finish, do so with a flourish. Bow crisply. That way, if your enemy were watching, he would be intimidated.

Depending on the length and type of technique, you could become totally winded by the addition of this facet of the training. The idea is to use up your anger in practice. Repeat the form as many times as necessary, until you are exhausted, if need be. Every time you do it, the technique becomes better and the anger becomes less. Eventually you will no longer need to psyche yourself up. You will need only to think of the trigger word. This single technique will enhance your practice a hundredfold.

It is really not very difficult to perform this trick. Almost everyone has had, or heard of, an imaginary friend in childhood. At first it might be hard to face an unpleasant memory or frightening experience. But all psychologists and shamen agree that the fear must eventually be faced and overcome, either by "flooding" (sudden inescapable confrontation) or "immersion" (gradual examination and understanding). Otherwise, strong emotions are either consciously suppressed or subconsciously repressed leading to psychological disorders.

Eventually, after decades or a lifetime of practice, one

comes to understand that there are no enemies but those we make in our own minds. At that point, the imaginary enemy becomes an ally, since, even from the first, it was merely a representative facet of one's own self. Every major religion and philosophy teaches that anger directed at another is merely the ego condemning some aspect of its own personality with which it disagrees. Anger is the child of frustration and is the last resort of the ignorant. The best fighter is not angry.

THE PRINCIPLES OF MAGIC

Magic—sleight of hand, prestidigitation, and all manner of conjuring—is based on five basic principles that are encompassed and historically taught as the Lost Track form, or *Mi Lu kata,* of ninjitsu. In Japanese, *mi* is "hidden, secret, unfathomable"; *lu* is "track, path, guidance." This kata is divided into elemental sections relating to the cosmology of the ancients, each of which is further broken down into subdivisions.

1. Angle Method. If one regards invisibility as maintaining a lack of presence rather than achieving it, the basis of this principle is apparent. In sleight of hand it is said, "If I can see it, you can't." This means that an object cupped in the palm, with the back of the hand to the spectator, is unseeable and will remain so unless the angle is changed to reveal it. So it is with punches: The uppercut slides up the enemy's chest, making it impossible for him to see unless he looks down his nose.

2. Blinding Method. There is an old ninjitsu saying: "A grain of sand in the eye can hide a mountain." If the enemy closes his eyes or looks away, then, again, everything vanishes. In stage magic, this may take the form of creating clouds of smoke to conceal some action. In combat, anything that can be thrown toward the enemy's face to make him flinch or blink long enough for the Ninja either to close the gap and strike him or duck out of sight is classified in this category.

3. Misdirection Method. An ancient sleight-of-hand proverb states that to conceal a movement of one hand, move both hands. Tactically, this means simultaneously striking at two targets, believing that the enemy can only block one effectively. It also includes attracting the enemy's attention to one area and then striking with the other hand. This is sometimes referred to as a "sucker punch." Furthermore, the practice of feinting many simple attacks to gauge the enemy reaction falls into this division.

4. Scarf Method. An invaluable aid for many magicians is a large silk scarf, beneath which he can create the illusion of space and shape. From this principle is derived the Japanese technique of *Ametori-No-Jitsu,* in which the Ninja filled his uniform with straw or suspended it in such a way that the enemy thought he was standing in one place, while actually he had already escaped or was hiding in ambush.

5. Mind Method. By making a conscientious study of the psychology of the human mind, the Ninja was able to play on the emotions of an enemy by means of the five feelings and five desires. The art of *Hsi Men Jitsu* ("Way of the Mind Gate") was part of the curriculum of every agent. This not only made him less susceptible to such trickery himself, but enabled him to manipulate the enemy in a manner similar to that of a stage hypnotist with a volunteer from the audience.

It was stated at the outset that this text would include no techniques which would enable the practitioner to control the mind of the enemy or any other human being, but only those whereby one might learn to control oneself. This ability often makes the Ninja appear to possess some secret power or hidden strength that enables him to perform amazing feats and seeming miracles. But anyone, with practice and diligent effort, can duplicate these efforts or any others which may be desired.

No one else has the power to make our wishes come true for us, but each of us has the power to make our own wishes come true. In fact, we are the only ones in a position to do so, since we are the only ones who know the true intent of the wish or prayer, and we must decide when the conditions of the contract have been satisfied.

Knowledge is the key. If one knows what to do, and how

to do it, the impossible can be made to seem easy and commonplace. One of the benefits of such knowledge is confidence. This is not an air of arrogance, but of determination and understanding. And a part of that confidence—the feeling that one can defend oneself from physical attack—is developed by applying the magic principles to combat.

The techniques of Mi Lu kata are not pretty or elaborate. They are simple and effective, requiring little strength and enabling the adept to engage the enemy or disappear. One can anticipate the enemy move, getting the jump on him by being able to predict the outcome; or one can trick him into making the move desired, also determining the outcome. The most fundamental and difficult to master of the techniques found here is the spin-back pivot, which enables the practitioner not only to become invisible to the enemy, but also to remain so indefinitely. Thus it is the basis of ninjitsu.

"A man cannot hit what he cannot see," and "the tiger cannot strike he who rides his back," are two ancient precepts of the art of invisibility. They are also the basic strategy of the warrior-mystic Ninja. The warrior-mystic loves life, not just his own, but also that of the enemy, whom he views as merely misinformed or misguided in most cases; but at the same time, he is quite capable of fighting or of vanishing. The man of peace knows that it takes two to make a conflict; therefore he retires, waiting patiently for the enemy to realize the error of his ways. Ninja do not fight wars. Knowing that one man in the right place at the right time can change the course of history, the Ninja seek out those individuals who cause the innocent to be slaughtered on the battlefield and stop them. Normally, however, they do not interfere in the affairs of men—unless, of course, they stray too far from the true path.

There are nine "sucker punches" in the Lost Track form, any one of which is guaranteed to distract the enemy long enough to allow the student to get in the first strike or disappear. These punches are taught to all members of the Black Dragon Fighting Society and are revealed here for the first time.

CEREMONIAL BOW

"The greatest warrior wins without fighting."

Sun Tzu

In any formal match, the opponents traditionally begin by bowing to each other. This is often interpreted as a sign of respect for each other's skill and ability. It is also the case that a good fighter, having studied extensively, will be aware of the many styles and systems; therefore he will be able to classify an adversary according to his stance and preparatory steps. Naturally, if one were attacked in an ambush, there would be no time for such pleasantries; but a true master could avoid such an attack, and still warn his assailants by a gesture or password.

In Chinese cosmology, the closed right fist represents Yang, the positive force, while the left symbolizes Yin, the encircling force. When the left palm covers the right fist, that is known as the Sign of Eternity (Figure 25), which means that the agent possesses secret knowledge. Other fighters who recognize this sign do not contend further, unless they believe themselves to be of equal or greater skill. In one sense this is because they might consider themselves "brothers of the same school"; in another sense, they would be foolish to fight with a professional, whose hands are considered lethal weapons.

Always end the kata with the same bow, to prove to any onlookers that you did know what you were doing, and that the enemy was fairly warned before he killed himself by forcing the fight.

Figure 25.

Figure 26.

RAISING THE CURTAIN

From the bow, the Ninja steps back with his left foot and folds his arms over his chest defensively (Figure 26). This is called the *kasumi* stance. The scarf application of this technique is as follows: Using a cape or blanket, lay the cloth across the chest and fold the arms as shown. To the observer it appears that the cape is draped on the shoulders and the edges are wrapped about the body, as would be customary. This is the illusion of form within the scarf.

Figure 27.

DRAGON-SPREAD WINGS

The Ninja spreads his arms in a slow, dramatic motion, holding the corners of the cloth by the fingertips, to present a solid sheet (Figure 27). To an observer it would seem that the Ninja has opened his cape to make himself appear larger. This is a psychological ploy as well, an intimidating gesture that may be sufficient in itself to dissuade further conflict. In reality, the cape now hangs inbetween the combatants, instead of around the agent. From this stance, it can be thrown over the enemy's head, blinding him while you escape.

Figure 28.

HALF STEP

In combat, half of the battle involves closing the gap between the fighters safely, in order to bring the enemy within striking range. The half step employs the misdirection method, and relies on the fact that movement attracts the eye. The enemy is compelled to watch both of your hands, since they represent the potential strike. Spread your hands and assume the Dragon-Spread Wings, placing your hands at opposite sides of the enemy's vision. Take advantage of this split focus of attention, and simultaneously slide the rear foot quietly behind the lead, thereby advancing one half step unseen. Snap-kick the enemy in the groin, which is now in range (Figure 28).

Figure 29.

Application of the Half Step

As the enemy is distracted by the movement of the arms, he does not see the subtle sliding forward of the rear foot, which advances the Ninja one half step. It is an old boxing maxim that to strike the head, one should take a full step; to strike the body, only one half step (Figure 29).

Before the enemy can react to the advance, the Ninja snaps out with a front kick to the groin (Figure 30). Impact may be made with the ball of the foot for maximum speed, or with the heel in the Dragon Stamp kick. Likewise, alternative targets are anywhere from the solar plexus down along the centerline of the body.

Figure 30.

Figure 31.

DOUBLE FRONT SNAP-KICK

Without putting the lead foot down from the half step, snap-kick again, striking the enemy's head as he falls forward as a result of the first kick to the midsection (Figure 31). This devastating double attack is performed in a quick staccato fashion and is an example of the principle of feinting. Even if the first attack is blocked, the second usually will get through.

Figure 32.

SWORD HAND

Some styles of karate insist that a proper snap-kick is only performed when the foot returns to its original position. That is fine for forms, but in most cases, especially high kicks, the natural tendency is to fall forward. The Ninja takes advantage of this momentum to further advance on the enemy. Maintaining a firm guard with his left hand to deflect any attack by the enemy, the agent strikes down diagonally onto the side of the enemy's neck with a vertical chopping action of his right hand (Figure 32). The intent is to stun the enemy by hitting the large muscle on the side of the neck, or to break the collarbone. Either way, this is a disabling blow.

Figure 33.

Application of Double Front Snap-Kick and Follow-Up Sword Hand

In Japanese, kicking the enemy chin with the ball of the foot is called *ago-geri,* literally, "chin-kick." It is quite capable of rendering the enemy unconscious or killing him due to the whiplash type of injury inflicted by snapping the head violently backward. Few Ninja kick above the waist level, since high kicks require more balance. In this case, the first kick has already brought the target down to the proper height (Figure 33).

The logical follow through for any snap-kick is the vertical chop. Even if the kick misses, by stepping down and forward with it, one gains enough ground to reach the enemy's head and the momentum adds weight to the impact. The vertical chop may be performed to the outside line as shown (Figure 34), or inside, by deflecting the enemy arm aside.

Figure 34.

Figure 35.

TEARING DOWN THE DOOR

Having disposed of the first adversary, the Ninja then confronts the second, who immediately steps in. He leans back slightly to avoid the imagined attack and raises both hands defensively. He then steps forward into the attack by taking a full step with his right foot (Figure 35). Historically, this action is derived from simultaneously holding a door and jamming it with the foot.

Figure 36.

ENTANGLING ARMS

Swing the arms in a wide counterclockwise arc, keeping the hands an equal distance apart, as if wiping a large mirror with a cloth (Figure 36). This action effectively sweeps aside any linear attack made by the enemy. The scarf application is to cast the blanket over the enemy's head from the side. Rock back slightly as you circle the arms, thereby withdrawing before the intended strike while pressing the enemy attack down and to the side. The arms act to entangle the enemy's arms and forestall him.

Figure 37.

Application of Entangling Arms

The arms, working together, deflect and engage the enemy, preventing him from making an effective strike. Try to make his arm cross the line of engagement. That is, try to get his arm between the two of you, where it will interfere with his intended tactics (Figure 37). This will also tend to confuse him and disrupt his balance. Remember, a force of one thousand pounds can be turned by four ounces.

Figure 38.

PUSHING THE DOOR

Rock forward over the leading leg as you push forward
from the rear hip with both hands, as if closing a door. Push
slightly upward in an effort to "uproot" the enemy (Figure
38). This double palm push with shoulders square enables the
practitioner to withstand a powerful force directed against
him. Again, the analogy is that of holding a doorway closed.
Focus the chi to the front and direct it through the palms.

Figure 39.

Application of Pushing the Door

In this instance, the left hand acts as the *soe-te,* or "entangling arm," while the right is called *mu-te,* the "striking arm." In the continuation of this action, the enemy's left arm is carried down and to the Ninja's left; again, across the line of engagement. Crossing one of the enemy's arms atop the other to trap him is called *juji-uke.* By rocking forward with the push, one can shove the enemy aside (Figure 39).

Figure 40.

Figure 41.

DRAGON-TAIL KICK

The spinning-back leg sweep is one of the simplest and most effective of any in the martial arts. It illustrates the angle method, since the Ninja drops out of sight before taking down the enemy. From the double-palm push, drop to all fours and extend the left leg (Figure 40). Pivot on the

Figure 42.

right knee, using the hands for balance, and swing the left leg 180 degrees to the rear (Figure 41). Used properly, this leg sweep knocks the enemy's legs out from under him (Figure 42).

Figure 43.

SAND IN THE EYES

Following the Dragon-Tail kick, you are now facing in the opposite direction from where you started, in a low kneeling stance. While this limits the angles from which the enemy can strike you, it also gives him the advantage of higher ground. Using the blinding method, the Ninja scoops a handful of sand in each fist as the enemy approaches (Figure 43). Then, pushing off with a rear leg, the Ninja

Figure 44.

throws both hands upward toward the enemy's face as he stands, launching the sand into his eyes (Figure 44). This technique is so effective that even if no powder or sand is thrown, the enemy will still flinch in an instinctive reaction to protect the eyes. This technique permits the agent either to strike while the enemy is blinded and at a disadvantage, or to disappear.

Figure 45.

Application of Sand in the Eyes

Dropping low to avoid any attack by the advancing enemy, the Ninja grabs two fistfuls of sand as his weapon (Figure 45).

Rising quickly, he uses an underhand toss to throw the missiles into the enemy's face (Figure 46). With very little

Figure 46.

practice this can be an incredibly effective self-defense technique for even the most passive student. There is hardly a man alive that can block a handful of sand. Even if he tries, his attention is diverted from the assault long enough to permit the prudent Ninja to flee.

Figure 47.

MI LU STEP (PIVOT)

The principle of getting behind the enemy in order to be invisible to him is another example of the angle method. The enemy cannot hit what he cannot see. This step is one way of turning the corner to evade the enemy attack. From the previous position with the right foot forward, take one full step straight ahead with arms raised for balance (Figure 47). When performed in combat this will place you shoulder to shoulder with the enemy, facing in opposite directions.

Figure 48.

Application of the Mi Lu Step

The Ninja has stepped through the narrow gap between himself and the enemy while pivoting on the ball of the lead foot, and is now halfway behind the enemy (Figure 48). In order to pass his enemy, he turned his back to him during the second in which the enemy's eyes were closed by his instinctive blinking at the sand or pebbles thrown in his face.

Figure 49.

SPIN-BACK PIVOT

From the previous pose, pivot clockwise on the toes of the left foot, bringing the right foot near the left ankle without setting it down. Step out to the right with the right foot into a horse stance for balance, and bring the arms up, either defensively or to strike the enemy from behind (Figure 49). This is sometimes known as the boxing step, or the *hsiao pu*, ("melting/vanishing step"). It places the practitioner belly to back with the enemy.

Figure 50.

Application of the Spin-Back Pivot

The Ninja has stepped behind the enemy into a modified horse stance and strikes the enemy behind the ear with a sharp *shuto,* or sword-hand blow, to render him senseless. His shoulders are now square to those of the adversary and they are facing in the same direction (Figure 50). When fighting more than one opponent, this is also useful in providing a human shield between yourself and any remaining attackers.

Figure 51.

SCRAPING SIDEKICK

Following the previous technique, you are once again facing in the original starting direction. Strike out directly to the side (Figure 51). For instance, if you began facing north, this kick is aimed west. This is a low sidekick, intended to strike the enemy's leg just below the knee with the edge of the foot. This is a crippling blow in itself, but the Ninja adds to its effectiveness by falling forward with the kick so the blade of the foot scrapes painfully down the enemy's shin and the heel stamps down hard on the instep.

Figure 52.

Application of Scraping Sidekick

In this illustration, the enemy has been trapped by the Ninja's weight. This technique exemplifies the misdirection method, forcing the enemy to direct his attention to his foot, down and away from the intended target, his head. Note that the lead hand is carried low, in preparation for the backfist strike, and that the Ninja continues to lean away from the enemy as well as keep his lead shoulder toward him, to present as small a target as possible (Figure 52).

Figure 53.

BACKFIST

With the enemy's foot pinned to the ground, effectively trapping him to the spot, the Ninja whips out his leading hand to strike the enemy at the base of the skull with the back of the first two knuckles (Figure 53). This is a quick, snappy action designed to produce a sharp blow to the skull and stun the opponent. This is an easy punch to learn and is so effective and sneaky that it is illegal in Western boxing.

Figure 54.

Application of Backfist

When the enemy looks down, the Ninja shifts his weight over the forward leg to immobilize him and lashes out with the backfist strike. The rear hand remains near solar plexus level in a defensive mode (Figure 54). This technique works almost every time, but only once per opponent.

Figure 55.

DOUBLE BLOCK

At the end of the previous posture, you were facing forward, or north, in a wide horse stance, looking west, or to the left. In kata it is presumed that the next attacker steps up quickly, approaching perpendicular to your line of balance (an imaginary line running between the soles of the feet). A force acting along this line, from the side for example, has little effect; a force acting at 90 degrees to this line can easily push you over backward. This is a quick block covering a large area, using the arms alone (Figure 55).

Figure 56.

Application of Double Block

The left arm forms *chudan,* the middle block, as the right simultaneously performs *gedan,* the down block (Figure 56). This protects everything from the eyebrows to the groin, and clears the centerline. This movement is designed to give you a second to retreat or advance from a head-on attack.

Figure 57.

COIN TOSS

The Ninja were always lovers of peace, even in feudal times. When confronted by bandits on the road, they would sometimes resort to tossing a small bag of coins to the thief as a token payment. This "road tax" was cheap if it saved a fight. When the Ninja were being chased, the same stratagem often stopped less than enthusiastic guards, or caused passersby to impede the pursuit in their efforts to grab a few coins thrown into a crowd. Such a purse or pouch

Figure 58.

was often carried on the hip at waist level, where it could
easily be pulled free.

In the kata, this action begins by showing the coins in the
open palm as you step back with the left foot (Figure 57).
Once the enemy's attention is on the bag, throw it, or the
loose coins, upward into his face (Figure 58). This will cause
him to blink, thus representing both the blinding and psychological methods. This move is equally effective when done
as a single-hand sand throw, in which instance the hand
would be closed until the toss.

Figure 59.

Application of Coin Toss

As the enemy nears, the Ninja steps back to maintain the gap between himself and the enemy and to stay out of range. At the same time, his right hand reaches across to the left hip and takes hold of the "coin purse" (Figure 59). In the field, this may take the form of any easily opened container filled with powder, sand, or metal filings.

Figure 60.

Then the Ninja whips his palm upward and out to cast the coins or blinding powder into the enemy's face (Figure 60). A little practice with a handful of flour can make a warrior out of anyone. Again, this illustrates the blinding method in solo application. This is an extremely dirty trick which, if it fails, is almost certain to incite the enemy to fury and rage.

Figure 61.

HENG PU: CROSS STEP

Following the previous posture, one may elect to attack or withdraw from the field. In kata, we step away from the enemy by cross-stepping behind with the right foot (Figure 61). Since this is also an advance in the opposite direction, we strike out with the left backfist strike to the enemy's head. This is a snappy action from the elbow with the fist clenched at the second of impact. While this blow is often effective, the real purpose of the movement is to mask the action of the legs, which enables the Ninja to come within range.

Figure 62.

Application of Cross Step

In application against a single opponent, the Ninja closes the gap between the combatants by lashing out with his back-fist while surreptitiously cross-stepping in back, out of sight of the enemy. If begun from long range, as shown (Figure 62), the enemy can fairly easily see and deflect this strike. It is most effective if several advances are made first as probing attacks, and then this move is used to gain ground. Always strike as if sincerely trying to hit the enemy in the temple; it might work. In any event, he will not react to an obvious feint.

Figure 63.

SPIN BACKFIST

This is one of the most devastating strikes in ninjitsu. It is often seen even in the professional kick-boxing ring. From the cross-leg stance, pivot quickly on the balls of both feet, spinning 180 degrees to the rear. As you turn, move the head more swiftly than the body to sight in on the target; load the right elbow across the chest at shoulder level. If you are too close, strike with the elbow; if not, snap out the fist (Figure 63).

Figure 64.

Application of Spin Backfist

From the cross step, whip around to strike the enemy from an unexpected angle. One may use the backfist, as shown (Figure 64); or, if closer, the lateral elbow strike; or, by dropping low, a hammerfist to the liver, or reverse "Monkey Steals the Peach" strike to the groin. Keep the chin tucked into the shoulder for protection, and practice "spotting" (picking the target and fixing on it before unleashing the strike).

Figure 65.

BEAT-DOWN BLOCK

After the last position, you are facing east. Now look north over the left shoulder, and swing both arms together in a wide arc, as if turning a great wheel. Both hands make fists. As you turn, shift your weight from the right to the left foot, establishing that as the platform leg, preparatory to *zen kutsu dachi,* or the frontal stance (Figure 65). The intent is to beat down on the enemy attack, which is imagined as coming from the north. Both of the arms must move together for the follow-up technique.

Figure 66.

Application of Beat-Down Block

Regardless of the enemy attack, whip the arms over and down, striking forcibly with a hammerfist or inverted fist strike, to knock the enemy's arms down and to the side (Figure 66). The intent is not so much to block him as to break his arm. Thereafter one may open the fist and trap the enemy advance, thus opening the line of engagement.

Figure 67.

POWER PUNCH

Using the momentum of the arm-swinging, hurl the right fist in a hooking arc to strike the enemy's head in what is often known as a roundhouse punch. Add power to this strike by turning the shoulders forward, squaring them to the front of the enemy (Figure 67). If he evades by fading, or launches a secondary attack, this overhand beating action can also strike that aside; if not, the hit can take the form of a hook, or Tiger Claw fist.

Figure 68.

Application of Power Punch

Drive the right fist into the enemy strongly enough to knock aside any defense he may put up (Figure 68). In motion pictures, the hero often uses this punch, which employs all of his weight, as his finishing technique on an otherwise difficult opponent. Practice it a few times, imagining your worst enemy as the receiver. Take care not to throw your shoulder out or twist your torso too far.

Figure 69.

DOUBLE THUMB GOUGE

Following the previous strike, face north with the left foot forward. Assuming that the previous double strike merely beat aside the enemy defense, take advantage of the opening to step up with the right foot and drive both thumbs deep into the enemy's eyes. Grab hold of his ears and/or hair for a good grip on his head. *Kiai,* or scream, as you step forward and, if unmasked, make a ferocious face to frighten the enemy and make him flinch (Figure 69).

Figure 70.

KNEE STRIKE

If you are holding the enemy's head, lift the left knee and drive it against the skull to crush the face and finish him off (Figure 70). If the thumbs miss or you have only partial control of the enemy, drive the knee into the groin to break the pubic arch and effectively cripple him. This is an excellent close-in fighting technique, requiring little actual strength and having a profound effect.

Figure 71.

OPENING THE CURTAIN

This move is sometimes known as "Parting the Veil." Facing north with the hands palm up, describe two small circles in opposite directions, moving the hands from the hara level, where they ended in the previous movement, to eyebrow level. The hands separate as if parting the folds of a curtain to allow a performer to step on stage. The left foot is forward, having been set down gently after the knee strike. The body is square to the enemy, but slightly withdrawn in a defensive stance with 70 percent of the weight on the rear leg (Figure 71).

Figure 72.

Application of Opening the Curtain

This technique is very effective for opening the line of engagement between oneself and the opponent. As he advances with arms outstretched to grapple, drop low or fade back to reduce the area of your body that is vulnerable to attack. This is called "target denial." Swing the arms up in simultaneous mirror blocks to separate the enemy's arms and open his centerline for attack (Figure 72).

Figure 73.

MONKEY STEALS THE PEACH

This is the classical name for the upward groin slap. Drop to the right knee, swinging the arms like windmills to distract the enemy and deflect any defense he may offer. The left arm ends in *jodan,* the rising forearm block, protecting the head as you drop low and slide forward without stepping. The right arm swings up and back, circling from the shoulder. Turn the palm up as it swings between the enemy's feet to stun him (Figure 73).

Figure 74.

Application of Monkey Steals the Peach

Whip the arms as described and strike the enemy's groin with the open palm, fingers bent at the first joint in a Monkey Paw or Tiger Claw fist (Figure 74). The impact will lift the enemy off the ground. Those skilled in chi kung can direct energy up the *Ch'ueng Mo* channel of the body and stop the heart. Followers of the Iron Hand styles immediately clench their fists tightly, with a crushing grip, and jerk the hand sharply back to the near hip, effectively ripping away the genitals. Massive blood loss causes death.

TO FINISH

When you stand following the groin strike, draw your left foot back slightly and fold your arms across your chest, left over right. Lean back. You are now back in the original starting position, except you are exactly reversed, i.e., when you started the kata your right foot was forward, now your left foot is.

Start again from the beginning and perform every movement in the Mi Lu kata again, this time on the other side. In the past, one requirement for training as a Ninja was that the student be ambidextrous. By repeating the movements on the other side, one is able to react quickly to any attack, no matter which quarter it is launched from, and thus end the conflict decisively, with a minimum of technique and effort.

At the completion of the second, or "mirror," repetition, end by covering the right fist, folded around the thumb, with the left open palm to form the Sign of Eternity (Figure 25). This identifies the performer as one schooled in the secrets and mysteries of the Art, and possessed of deeper understanding than may be apparent to the casual observer.

Each of the techniques of the Lost Track form illustrates a specific principle of magical science. "If one wishes to disguise the movement of one hand, move both hands," is a canon of prestidigitation that illustrates simultaneous attack. "Sand in the eye can hide a mountain" embodies the method of blinding or flinching. "One cannot hit what one cannot see" is demonstrated by the angle method. "Feinting an attack to the head raises the enemy guard" is an example of misdirection. "The only thing to fear is fear itself" typifies the psychological or mind method. One might suspect that this system of fighting was developed by magicians. And it was—the warrior-mystics of ninjitsu.

9.
The Hidden Masters: Spirit Helpers

"The way is known to all, but not all know it."

When you obtained this book, it was because you were in search of occult power. It has been said, however, that no one may find such power without personal instruction from one skilled in the dark arts, and that is so. So how may we contact these secret teachers—if, indeed, we wish to pursue this quest? The answer is simple: we must follow their example.

True knowledge endures without regard for the sands of time, and the immutable laws of the universe carry each of us to our fate, whether we take notice or not. There are many paths to the Universal Mind, the Cosmic Consciousness. One may follow the Eightfold Path and grow; or one may embrace the Way of the Spiritual Devotee. All paths lead to the dwelling place of Vishnu, who knows all, sees all, and tells all. At this level of mind, anything is possible.

If we seek to become one with Nature, then, and to experience communion with this All-Wise Consciousness, we must concede that we conceive of it as being "outside" of ourselves. At that point we feel loneliness, which causes us to seek the counsel of others. Most people are motivated by self-interest, however; there are those who would take advantage of this motivation. So finally we are left completely abandoned. Every living being passes through this test of self-doubt. This is the Dark Night of the Soul, when one decides between life and death and finds the inner strength, with or without "help."

"I have no friend; I make my mind my friend." These words are taught in Zen meditation and are part of the Japanese creed of the samurai. The Ninja carry this one step further with Hsi Men Jitsu, the Chinese art of psychology. Hsi Men Jitsu teaches that there are three facets of every personality. Dr. Eric Berne called them *child, adult,* and *internalized parent.* The ancients referred to them as *heaven, earth,* and *man (shen, ch'i,* and *ching).* The Hidden Masters are the high self, the jonin, the upper man, the internalized mores and behaviors we have learned from authority figures.

Invoking and communicating with the Hidden Masters serves three functions: First, it enables one to act as an actual parent, thus promoting survival of the race; second, it makes many responses automatic, in accordance with the principle of cause and effect; and third, the spirit helper acts as a counsel and guide when we are lost, a friend when we are alone, and a teacher of secret knowledge. Everyone has such an ally who can be trusted completely and consulted on any question.

The purpose of the exercises in this book is to calm the "lower" self, the chakras or energy centers of the body that are concerned only with gratification of the physical desires: air, water, food, shelter, sex. In so doing, the energy of the body can be raised and, with it, the level of consciousness. When this has been accomplished, we become sensitive to the forces of Nature and can act in accordance with the laws of the universe.

To accomplish this, one need only begin. It may require more effort for some than others, and it may need to be attempted several times, even at different ages, to effect a sufficient rapport with the alter ego. Nevertheless it can be done. It has been done before, and will be done again.

Many cultures have secret ceremonies whereby one may

find or summon one's spiritual advisor; and, of course, everyone has a different concept of the appearance and/or mode of communication of this personage. For most, it is an automatic and unconscious process, but when coupled with the power of imagination, it becomes a powerful ally. It may be the memory of a beloved relative that appears to counsel us, or a combination of several people who have had a powerful or guiding influence, or even a figure from history. It may even be the little voice of our conscience which keeps us out of trouble most of the time, that whispers in our ear. As long as we are aware of the benevolent and guiding nature of these advisors, we may be assured of their assistance and support. The more frequently they are consulted, the more influence they can have and the greater the ease with which they may be contacted.

History and experience have shown that whatever form these imaginary friends take, they have certain common characteristics. Since they represent authority figures, all are firm and honest in their advice and directions. Since they are the idealized creation of a teacher or sage, they are never upset or angry; and their explanations, or the flashes of insight that they provide, fully answer and explain any question. This invariably has a calming effect on the practitioner and helps to allay any fears or anxiety that may be present. Lastly, since they are friends, they possess a sense of irony and humor. This enables us to see ourselves as others see us, and realize that most of our problems are self-induced and really of little consequence in the scheme of the universe. This leads to humility.

In the 1920s and '30s, the United States was inundated by spiritualists and mediums who claimed miraculous curative powers far beyond those of mortal men. They possessed, or so the story goes, a "spirit guide" from beyond this human plane, with whom they communicated while in a deep trance-like state. During these manifestations, the spirit guide was able to speak through the medium's voice, although the voices of each were distinctly dissimilar. We shall not attempt so profound a materialization at this juncture, but it should be noted that these mediums were merely persons who publicly acknowledged their imaginary friend.

There are hundreds of meditation techniques that help one contact one's spirit ally. Each relies on artificially altering the chemical state of the blood, either by deep breathing (hyperventilating) or holding the breath (hypoventilating). Each must be practiced carefully, lest the increased oxygen in the bloodstream make one conscious of the heartbeat. In many cases, this leads to anxiety; but that is easily calmed by simply holding the breath for a moment. Charlatans frequently insist that the resulting phenomenon is the result of some manipulation of their own, when in fact it is a simple physiological effect.

We present only the most rudimentary method here, one which, practiced patiently over a long period, will lead the curious to discover any helping agent that may be required. Rudyard Kipling wrote, "There is a certain calming influence that one may experience by the mere assumption of a comfortable position and the slow repetition of one's name." Likewise, such a practice also develops an awareness and understanding of Self. But before one requests of the Hidden Masters an ally—one who may act as sentry, scout, or spy, who is in contact with the Universal Mind of all mankind, and who has access to all things and all knowledge, hidden or revealed—one must make some preparation.

The degree of detail which is attributed to the ally contributes greatly to its realism and subsequent effectiveness; nevertheless one should not become so enamored of the fantasy relationship that it takes precedence over reality. Instead, one should be like a child making believe, pretending; one should suspend for a few moments the press of everyday life. This allows a certain surcease from the crush of responsibility, and that is called "reducing stress."

You may decide beforehand what type of advisor you desire, and prepare sketches or descriptive poetry, all of which enhance the experience. But in the end, it is the subconscious mind that determines the form you will perceive. If it matches or is similar to your preconceived image, then you already possess significant personal insight and self-knowledge. If not, then the high self will most often be the counterpoint of the child facet of your personality, thereby balancing the Yin and Yang in the adult self which must function in the real world.

Lie down in a comfortable position, so that all parts of the body are equally supported. Close your eyes. Become aware of the sounds around you. Do not be distracted by them, just be aware. Inhale deeply and fully, without strain, as you mentally count, "one, two, three, four." Hold the inhalation for the count of two. Relax and let the air flow easily out of the lungs as you count, "one, two, three, four." Hold the exhalation for the count of two. Repeat three times.

At first, the speed of the count will reflect your conscious state of mind. Later it will synchronize with the heartbeat. Finally it will regulate the heartbeat. When holding the breath in, do not constrict the muscles of the throat; this damages the blood vessels in the neck and face. On the exhalation, push the air out with the hara.

Think of the most pleasant experience you have ever had. Take three deep breaths and as you exhale each time, count backward from three to one. This is a deepening exercise that enables one to develop a more contemplative state. Furthermore it focuses the attention on the breathing, which helps to elicit what some Boston researchers have described as the "relaxation response" present in all humans. Feel the relaxation in your body. Any sounds that you may hear do not distract you from this contemplation. If left to random chance, most people at this stage drift easily into a light sleep.

The Ninja have a saying: "All men have three names: the one they are called, the one they are known by, and the one they share with no one else." So it is with the spirit helper. Having decided to contact this personage, we may do so leisurely, waiting for its appearance, at which time it will be recognized and subsequently named. Alternatively, you may seek to contact a specific entity, in which event the procedure now requires that you speak the name you have chosen. Repeat it three times, softly. This will be your own personal "mantra"; you are not to tell anyone else this mantra, since to do so invites comparison and/or criticism from those less imaginative.

Communication with the alter ego that you have contacted may take many forms, verbal, visual, or kinesthetic. It may even take the form of telepathy, since it is a dialogue of two minds.

> *When you are alone, or troubled, or need a help-*
> *ing hand*
> *Close your eyes and think of me and speak my*
> *name out loud*
> *And I will come.*
> *Look for me in the sky of a summer day,*
> *Listen for the sound of my footsteps on the path,*
> *Lift the rock and I am there.*
>
> —Cheyenne Indian chant

Postscript

"There is no secret except in the mind of the seeker."

It has always seemed that the masters perform with ease things which we mere mortals find inconceivable. They know the "trick"; that is what makes them mystics. To employ that knowledge properly is to be a warrior. That means accepting responsibility for one's actions. To kill is easy, and to win is easy; one need only cheat. One need only have the will to accomplish anything. But not cheating—that is what separates mankind from man-beast. To members of the animal kingdom, every situation is life or death. Only man can differentiate between good and evil, discriminating whether he must use all his powers to survive, or whether what is transpiring is merely the blustering of the ego; either his own or another's.

The mood of the warrior is one of waiting; he waits for time and circumstance to stir his will. He is patient and tolerant. To occupy himself, he trains to perfect his skill, his *kung fu* ("ability"). He studies to increase his understanding of himself and others, knowing them to be one and the same. He is a man of peace who fights like ten tigers. He is the keeper of the secret knowledge. He is the warrior-mystic, who, in silence so deadly, destroys the enemy unseen. He is the Ninja.

Thus the Game can begin. To play is simple: One merely follows one's true nature, which is beyond illusion or delusion. One strives for the perfection of character by fostering the spirit of effort. One defends the paths of truth, honoring the principles of etiquette and guarding against impetuous courage. One acquires merit by doing good works, seeking to discover new means and new companions with which to enjoy the quest. There is no enlightenment outside of oneself. One may play the Game or ignore it. It goes on forever, regardless.

NOTES

NOTES

NOTES

NOTES

NOTES

NOTES

NOTES

NOTES

NOTES

NOTES

NOTES

Martial Arts Books Ordering Information

Ask for any of the books listed below at your bookstore. Or to order direct from the publisher, call 1-800-447-BOOK (MasterCard or Visa), or send a check or money order for the books purchased (plus $4.00 shipping and handling for the first book ordered and 75¢ for each additional book) to Carol Publishing Group, 120 Enterprise Avenue, Dept. 50997, Secaucus, NJ 07094.

Aikido Complete
by Yoshimitsu Yamada
Oversized 7" x 10", illustrated with step-by-step photographs throughout
$9.95 paper   0-8065-0914-7

Forbidden Fighting Techniques of the Ninja by Ashida Kim
Oversized 8 1/2" x 11", illustrated with step-by-step photographs throughout
$9.95 paper   0-8065-0957-0

From Bruce Lee to the Ninjas: Martial Arts Movies by Richard Meyers, Amy Harlib, Bill and Karen Palmer
Oversized 8 1/2" x 11", illustrated with photographs throughout
$14.95 paper   0-8065-1009-9

The Invisible Ninja
by Ashida Kim
Illustrated with step-by-step photographs throughout
$9.95 paper   0-8065-1873-1

Jiu Jitsu Complete by Kiyose Nakae
Illustrated with step-by-step drawings throughout
$9.95 paper   0-8065-0418-8

How To Become a Ninja: Secrets From Ashida Kim's Training Camp
by Anonymous
Illustrated with step-by-step photographs throughout
$9.95 paper   0-8065-1558-9

Ninja Mind Control by Ashida Kim
Illustrated with step-by-step photographs throughout
$8.95 paper   0-8065-0997-X

Ninja Training Manual: Self-Defense and Fighting Secrets
by Christopher Hunter
Illustrated with step-by-step photographs throughout
$8.95 paper   0-8065-1781-6

Secrets of the Ninja by Ashida Kim
Illustrated with step-by-step photographs throughout
$10.95 paper   0-8065-0866-3

Ultimate Aikido: Secrets of Self-Defense and Inner Power by Yoshimitsu Yamada, with Steven Pimsler
Oversized 8 1/2" x 11", illustrated with step-by-step photographs throughout
$17.95 paper   0-8065-1566-X

(Prices subject to change; books subject to availability)